Highest Praise for ROBERT L. DILENSCHNEIDER and His Groundbreaking Books

DECISIONS
Practical Advice from 23 Men and Women Who Shaped the World

"Decision making and problem solving
made easy, now that's good news!"
—**Ernie Anastos,** Emmy award–winning
news anchor, WNYW-TV

"*Decisions* delivers sound advice wrapped in often
little-known stories of a broad range of people from
JFK to Ignaz Semmelweis. Fun to read and sound."
—**Fay Vincent,** former commissioner
of Major League Baseball

"There is no wiser counsel in business and much else
besides than Bob Dilenschneider. This supremely thoughtful
book will help any reader to think more clearly about
the decisions they face and, crucially, about the contexts
in which those decisions must be made."
—**Bill Emmott,** former editor in chief, *The Economist*

"Upgrade your daily decisions with the wisdom of two
dozen renowned influencers who changed history."
—**Mehmet Oz, M.D.,** Emmy Award-winning host of
The Dr. Oz Show and *New York Times* bestselling
author of *You: The Owner's Manual*

"Robert L. Dilenschneider's *Decisions* is a truly inspiring book
about how to become a leader. He is a masterful storyteller.
Every page is full of inspiration. Highly recommended!"
—**Douglas Brinkley,** CNN Presidential Historian and
New York Times ⸻⸻⸻⸻⸻⸻ *Moonshot:*
John F. ⸻⸻

"Dilenschneider gives the lie to the perception
that productivity declines after age 50."
—Rush Limbaugh

"The best career advice you can get
from one of the best in the business."
—Lou Dobbs

THE CRITICAL FIRST YEARS OF
YOUR PROFESSIONAL LIFE

"Dilenschneider, a savvy strategic thinker, has guided thousands
of highly successful people. Whether the economy is weak or
strong, he will help you navigate through the changing tides."
—Maria Bartiromo

"Dilenschneider offers practical advice on how young
people can take charge of their careers . . . A vital
resource for those involved with recruiting, motivating
or managing the future leaders of America."
—Norman R. Augustine, chairman and CEO,
Lockheed Martin Corporation,
and author of *Augustine's Laws*

"An insightful, idea-laden, practical guide
that will be valuable to young professionals."
—Stephen A. Greyser, Richard P. Chapman Professor
of Business Administration, Harvard Business School

"Dilenschneider shares strategic
advice and years of tested experience."
—Rev. Theodore M. Hesburgh, C.S.C.,
President Emeritus, University of Notre Dame

"This book should be essential reading for young
people starting out on a business career."
—Henry Kaufman, Henry Kaufman & Company

Books by ROBERT L. DILENSCHNEIDER

The Critical First Years of Your Professional Life★

50 Plus!★

Decisions★

The Critical 2nd Phase of Your Professional Life

Power and Influence

Civility in America

Public Relations Handbook

A Briefing for Leaders

The AMA Handbook of Public Relations

A Time for Heroes

Values for a New Generation

On Power

The Men of St. Charles

The Corporate Communications Bible

The Hero's Way

★Available from Kensington Publishing Corp.

PRACTICAL
ADVICE FROM
23 MEN AND
WOMEN WHO
SHAPED THE
WORLD

DECISIONS

ROBERT L. DILENSCHNEIDER

Foreword by STEVE FORBES
Afterword by KLAUS SCHWAB

CITADEL PRESS
Kensington Publishing Corp.
www.kensingtonbooks.com

CITADEL PRESS BOOKS are published by

Kensington Publishing Corp.
119 West 40th Street
New York, NY 10018

All Kensington titles, imprints, and distributed lines are available at special quantity discounts for bulk purchases for sales promotions, premiums, fund-raising, educational, or institutional use.

Special book excerpts or customized printings can also be created to fit specific needs. For details, write or phone the office of the Kensington sales manager: Kensington Publishing Corp., 119 West 40th Street, New York, NY 10018, attn: Sales Department; phone 1-800-221-2647.

ISBN-13: 978-0-8065-4052-8
ISBN-10: 0-8065-4052-4

First Citadel hardcover printing: January 2020

10 9 8 7 6 5 4 3 2 1

Printed in the United States of America

Electronic edition:

ISBN-13: 978-0-8065-4053-5 (e-book)
ISBN-10: 0-8065-4053-2 (e-book)

To my wife Jan,
the best decision I ever made

CONTENTS

Foreword *by Steve Forbes*   xi

Introduction   1

Part One: War and Peace
   Chapter 1: Harry Truman   11
   Chapter 2: Pablo Picasso   23
   Chapter 3: Elie Wiesel   36
   Chapter 4: Mahatma Gandhi, Dag Hammarskjöld   48
   Chapter 5: Margaret Thatcher   60
   Chapter 6: Joan of Arc   72

Part Two: Commerce and Invention
   Chapter 7: Johann Gutenberg   83
   Chapter 8: A. P. Giannini   95
   Chapter 9: Henry Ford   102
   Chapter 10: Howard Johnson   107

Part Three: Science
   Chapter 11: Alexander Fleming, Louis Pasteur,
      Ignaz Semmelweis   119
   Chapter 12: Marie Curie   128
   Chapter 13: Rachel Carson   137

Part Four: Breaking Boundaries
   Chapter 14: Hannibal, Julius Caesar, John Kennedy   151
   Chapter 15: Abraham Lincoln   163
   Chapter 16: Muhammad Ali   174

Chapter 17: Martin Luther 191
Chapter 18: Malala Yousafzai 205

Afterword *by Klaus Schwab* 211
Acknowledgments 215
Index 217

FOREWORD
by Steve Forbes

Decisions! Decisions!

We make countless numbers of them each day, most of them mundane and routine. But then there are those with consequences of varying degree: preparing a presentation; hiring and firing; putting together a budget; deciding on a major capital expenditure; starting a business; whether or not to propose marriage or accept/reject such a proposal; how best to perform a surgery if you're a physician; what experiments to pursue if you're in science or medicine; choosing a career or deciding on a new direction for your professional life; putting your physical safety on the line for a cause and on and on.

How best approach an impending decision of importance? It's an art, not a science, as this must-have book makes clear. There are times when you don't have the luxury of contemplation and must act with incomplete information, when there are no clear choices. Some leaders say they may go by their gut. But as Bob Dilenschneider illustrates, the "gut" is shaped by all previous experience and learning. It is not a blank slate.

Good decision-making requires discipline, as well as an ability to weigh an array of facts, even when they are seemingly contradictory. It requires being receptive for advice—only the ignorantly arrogant think they always know what they need to know—and when necessary, asking for it as a means to "give ownership" to those giving it, even if you don't take all or even a part of it.

And how to weigh the consequences of an act! What is humbling is that there is many a time where that is impossible, as Dilenschneider's chapters on Gutenberg and Luther graphically make clear. And, of course, there are moments when "the decider" (to use former President George Bush's appellation) knows full well the momentousness of a particular course of action, most famously Caesar crossing the Rubicon River, which he recognized would trigger civil war.

When it comes to deciding, there is no end of tips and guidelines for seemingly any and every situation.

What makes this book so valuable is that Dilenschneider, who has spent a lifetime counseling individuals and organizations on effective communications and crisis management, and in doing so, winning a legendary reputation as the penultimate "go-to guy" for strategizing and a source of sound counseling, knows the power of storytelling for compellingly making points that would otherwise be fairly useless abstractions.

Here he takes a wide range of individuals, most known but not all, and walks us through critical decisions they made that in various ways profoundly affected the world. He helpfully gives biographical thumbnail sketches and crucially lays out the *context* in which the person must act. Some are heart-wrenching as when Elie Wiesel must decide what to do about his father as they are about to be force-marched by Nazi guards from one death camp to another. Others are acts of courage in going forward despite personal losses and serious illness as was the case of Marie Curie.

Sometimes there are family pressures that can be formidable to overcome. Martin Luther's strong-willed father commanded that his son become a lawyer and work in the family mining business. The young Luther felt a calling to become a priest. Unwilling to face the issue directly, the man who would upend Europe and indeed the world and who never shirked a challenge, simply disappeared to a monastery, and only when ready to take his vows did he inform his father of what he had done!

We don't make decisions in a vacuum.

Motives? Some are noble and some seemingly mundane. Gutenberg wanted to make money. In his day, books were painstakingly handmade over a period of months. There was a market for more accessible knowledge. Gutenberg wanted to seize it, but it took him thirty years of experimentation to invent the printing press with movable type and to perfect the kind of paper that would be most practical. He didn't grasp that he had invented mass communications! And, more pressing for him, an unscrupulous lender yanked his business away just as Gutenberg was about to realize the fruits of his long labors. It would have been small consolation to him to know that no one would remember the moneylender while Gutenberg and his bibles would be immortal.

Having been in business for decades and keenly observing numerous leaders, as well as being a student of history, Dilenschneider is uniquely able to enrich his chapters with a texture and plausibility absent from those customary works offering how-to advice. The people he examines bring to life the lessons he then elucidates at the end of each chapter.

This is why this book is so valuable—you get to see "up close and personal" how decisions were made in numerous situations. Of course, times and circumstances are always changing. No two individual situations are exactly alike. But certainly there are chapters here that you will find useful to go back to for inspiration and help depending on the type of important decision you must make. As Mark Twain said, "History doesn't repeat itself, but it does rhyme."

DECISIONS

INTRODUCTION

THIS BOOK IS INTENDED to make your life better.

You make hundreds of decisions—some small, some significant—that mark your life. How you make those decisions is critical to your future.

The following pages capture vignettes about twenty-three individuals who made decisions that shaped the world, and whose stories stretch over time, from 218 B.C. to today.

Each chapter offers practical thinking on how these men and women made decisions. You can use their guidance in your daily life.

You will know these men and women. I selected them because (a) you will recognize them; and (b) they made decisions from which you and I can learn.

Most of you will know well the outcomes of the decisions made by these men and women. This book is intended to punctuate those results and to give you the context in which these actions were taken. Then you can take their lessons and ideas to make your daily life more productive and better.

Your life may become more enjoyable, too. I have noticed that many people dislike making decisions. They dread knowing that there are decisions to be faced. These people either avoid decisions entirely, or they are indecisive. This common behavior leads nowhere.

By reading the profiles in this book and absorbing and practicing the lessons they offer, you will have the tools you need to enjoy the decision-making process. When you enjoy doing something, you want to do it well. You want to keep doing it well and will constantly improve how you do it.

If you can make better decisions, your life will be better. And that is the reason I wrote this book, to offer you new ways to think about what you decide to do.

Every individual profiled sat alone—truly alone—and made their decisions. At the end of the day you are always alone when you make your decision, whether it is going for a job, spending your money, or the many other decisions that will shape your life.

Many of the decisions you take are easy and obvious. But some will not be. Some will change your life. And making the right decision will be of enormous value to you.

> Two roads diverged in a yellow wood,
> And sorry I could not travel both . . .
> —Robert Frost

So, like Robert Frost's narrator, I stood in my own yellow wood as I began writing this book about decisions. What should I do?

In my life (and my career), I have seen the importance of being able to make good, better, and even best decisions. I wanted to share the knowledge I have gained and the courage I have developed along the way, to help you improve your life and encourage others to do the same.

My goal is simple. But what direction should my book take to get there?

There is much to learn about decision-making. From art and literature, certainly. (What decision do you think Rodin's Thinker was trying to make? And besides Frost's narrator, what about such famous ditherers as Hamlet and *The Graduate*'s Benjamin?) Philosophy, psychology, business (decision trees), world religions (the Jesuit method of discernment), academia, and popular culture—all offer valuable perspectives. And if in doubt, there's always tossing a coin or reading tea leaves.

I have stood in this yellow wood before. I have written many books on business, communications, and careers, including two specifically on decision-making in those settings. Those books all reflected my experiences and my beliefs.

But this book is more personal.

Like you, I love history and try to learn from it. I also see how history is repeating itself in today's events and that being able to make good decisions is more crucial than ever.

So, because history has so much to teach us—and because history is formed by fellow human beings—I tell the stories of people because their decisions changed the world. These people were as real and as interesting as any of us, and their lives and decisions offer lessons to each one of us.

The book begins with Harry Truman who changed history in a way that shaped the world we live in today, a man I view as the epitome of a decision-maker. Truman was a self-educated, plain-spoken, unassuming man who never expected to get where he got in life but was graceful and grateful when he did. Yet this thirty-third American President made a breathtaking, heart-stopping, audacious decision in 1945 that reverberates worldwide to this day. Did Truman realize what would unfold in the twenty-first century? Probably not.

You and I probably do not realize what life and our lives and the lives of people close to us will be like twenty years from now. That said, we should at least try to think of what lies ahead and the effects that what we do will have on the future.

This book closes with Malala Yousafzai, a young Pakistani Muslim woman who embodies courage, who points the way to the future. Malala in 2012 literally faced death from the Taliban because of the way she and her family had bravely decided that her life should be lived—going to her local school. Educated at Oxford University and a Nobel Laureate, Malala continues her outspoken activism on behalf of educational and all rights for children. Her impact on the world is already palpable—what will the future bring?

How did Harry and Malala do what they did? What can the rest of us learn from them as we approach our own decisions large and small? What can we learn from the other visionary decision-makers whose stories I tell in this book?

And as you read on, you will meet and take ideas and advice from twenty-one other people, the likes of Pablo Picasso, Elie Wiesel, Mahatma Gandhi, Dag Hammarskjöld, Margaret Thatcher, Joan of Arc, Johann Gutenberg, A. P. Giannini, Henry Ford, Howard Johnson, Alexander Fleming, Louis Pasteur, Ignaz Semmelweis, Marie Curie, Rachel Carson, Hannibal Barca, Julius Caesar, John Kennedy, Abraham Lincoln, Muhammad Ali, and Martin Luther.

What will their lessons mean for you?

This book is not aimed at telling you all you need to know about these outstanding men and women. It is a book that puts you at their sides as they come to decisions that shaped the future of the world. And it will leave you with specific ways of thinking to make decisions important to you.

Each of us, like Caesar, has a Rubicon to cross. We all have a certain set of decisions to make that might, if properly done, lead to a better life for each of us and indeed a better world.

If you pursue the simple guidelines that are embedded in these stories of real people who made world-changing decisions, the minutes and hours and days—the years—that lie ahead for you will be more positive and exciting.

Believe me, it's worth the effort.

Like you, I make decisions all day long. I don't think about most of these decisions. I just make them. You do too. Reading this book, for example, instead of doing something else.

Many of our decisions are mundane and routine. They interest no one except you and those around you. When to get up, what to wear, what to eat for breakfast and so on. But even these mundane and routine decisions are not random. What to wear, for example, depends on what you will be doing that day.

Often, what I will be doing is working with clients of my communications counseling firm who—having made their own mundane and routine decisions earlier in the day—are now grappling with multi-faceted and compelling questions with very large human, corporate, industry, community, and global implications. These clients have a lot invested in making right and good decisions, and my long career has been devoted to helping this process go smoothly. (And it doesn't always.)

Of course, I have made plenty of personal decisions. Every one of us has. Some were enormously significant to me at the time and their import has faded, others remain foundational to my life and the people I love. Some decisions have been good; some, mistakes. I like to think that I have gotten better at decision-making as I have gotten older and have amassed more experience.

Along the way, I developed a fascination with decision-making, this very human process of sorting out, often in the midst of chaos and confusion or at least competing viewpoints, what should be done. I am sure that you think about this too, especially when a decision you make has a negative result.

Writing this book has strengthened my decision-making abilities. Considering individuals from as long ago as centuries B.C., to today, has given me insights I did not previously have. As I tell the stories of these people, I have tried to turn my insights into ideas and specific suggestions that will help you.

I hope this book inspires you. More practically, I hope it helps you reach a new and higher level of decision-making.

Even in the time it takes to read just a few sentences in this book, you and others around you will gain insights into how to make decisions that will shape the minutes, days, weeks, and years ahead.

★   ★   ★

Consider:

- Harry Truman and his decision to use the atomic bomb.
  - Once you have done it, you should never look back, but for the best outcome, continue.
- Pablo Picasso and his decision to paint the ultimate anti-war masterpiece, "Guernica."
  - Always step forward and use your talent to underscore the importance of doing the right thing.
- Elie Wiesel and his decision to use his life to keep the reality of the Holocaust alive.
  - Keep the decisions you need to make in perspective.
- Mahatma Gandhi/Dag Hammarskjöld and their decisions to pursue world peace.
  - Continually push nonviolent behavior that others will recognize and applaud because it is right.
- Margaret Thatcher and her decision to go to war.
  - Stick to your objective no matter what the barriers and problems.
- Joan of Arc and her decision to obey divine voices.
  - Do not be afraid to dream and let your imagination take hold of your actions.
- Johann Gutenberg and his decisions on using his new invention, movable type and the printing press.
  - Be clear about your goals.
- A. P. Giannini and his decision to focus his banking business.
  - Remember your start in life and the values you have learned and apply them in all you do.

- Henry Ford and his decision to pay his workers a living wage.
  - Make sure you listen to and take care of those who support you.
- Howard Johnson and his decision to franchise his restaurants.
  - Do your research and always be aware of the external conditions in which you operate.
- Alexander Fleming, Louis Pasteur, Ignaz Semmelweis, and their decisions to advance medicine and save lives.
  - Think outside the box. Involve others in your efforts.
- Marie Curie and her decision to persevere in the face of personal tragedy.
  - Do not hesitate to learn from others but always credit those with the original idea. If at all possible, do not make important decisions under pressure or following a negative event in your life.
- Rachel Carson and her decision to write *Silent Spring* and expose DDT.
  - Keep at it and no matter what distraction presents itself be determined in pursuit of your goals.
- Hannibal Barca, Julius Caesar, and John Kennedy, and their decisions to cross literal physical boundaries.
  - Always have a precise goal in mind and dedicate all you can to achieving that end.
- Abraham Lincoln and his decision to publish the Emancipation Proclamation.
  - Understand the value of patience.
- Muhammad Ali and his decisions to change his name and to resist the draft.
  - Develop your conscience.
- Martin Luther and his decision to defy the Catholic Church.
  - Follow your conscience and do what you think is

right. Do not be afraid of the unknown. Face it with
strength.
- Malala Yousafzai and her decision to stand up to the
  Taliban.
  - Learning from your earlier life is a key to your
    future. Never stop learning. Do not be reluctant to
    speak out on topics and issues that surround the
    commonweal.

George Bush famously said, "I'm the decider." It all comes
down to each one of us, individually, and this book should help
us get to a new and higher level of decision-making.

PART ONE
War and Peace

I

HARRY TRUMAN

The Buck Stops Here.
—HARRY TRUMAN

YEARS AFTER THE FACT, the atomic bombings of Hiroshima and Nagasaki in August 1945 stand in stark relief on history's timeline. An obvious turning point in history that meant life on earth has never been the same.

Also standing in stark relief is the seemingly lonely figure of the man who "made the decision" to take the step that, yes, effectively ended the carnage of World War II and brought a new kind of carnage. An immediate slew of horrendous death, injury, and destruction was unleashed by the bomb.

The permanent specter of total man-made destruction has stalked and haunted the world since 1945 and is possibly the most salient feature of modern life.

You and I all know that Harry S Truman was the man behind that decision to drop the bomb. That sentence almost seems to beg the use of the word "hiding" to modify "behind"— who would want to be tarred with such a decision? Wouldn't you want to be invisible or at least anonymous? Yet, in today's phrase, Truman owned that decision. He made it, he acknowledged, it and he never looked back.

And that sentence, though true on its face, also begs us to ask—How did he do it? How could he do it?

This book starts with Truman's story because of that decision. And because he was President, America has had a global impact that is still felt today. He left us a model for how we as a country must continue to provide the leadership for which these uncertain times call. I hope some of the thinking in this chapter will affect the thinking of big-time policy makers, and I intend to share what follows and indeed this entire book with heads of all the countries around the world.

The atomic bombs were dropped on August 6 and 9, 1945.

Barely four months earlier, on April 12, President Roosevelt had died and Vice President Truman had been sworn in to succeed him. Roosevelt had just begun his unprecedented fourth term and had this new VP (two other men had served with him in his previous twelve years in office). Accounts agree that FDR barely acknowledged Truman; in fact, didn't know him well, only met with him once during the 1944 campaign and twice after they were sworn in. Not the best move by a wartime leader who was visibly staggering under the load of his office, knowing he was near death.

History seems to tell us that Truman knew nothing about the existence of the bomb until about two weeks after he was sworn in; it's possible that he had been told of it, but only in a cursory way. (Even Truman seemed to contradict himself on this point.) In any event, the scant four months that he was in office was the only time that was available to Truman to ponder the question—hardly seems like enough.

A friend once told me that the most important decisions are made in the first 10 seconds of realizing that they have to be made. I have not been able to find, nor did I actually ask, the factual source to back up that assertion. But I quickly understood he did not mean that those decisions were superficially made, but that they were the product of a lifetime of preparation.

Truman had that lifetime of preparation, with many factors working for and against him. He was what I would call a "man of parts," a complex man. Every reader has a lifetime of preparation, some good, some insignificant. Consider the following for Truman.

- Intelligent though not well-educated, he knew how to take in new information, how to learn.
- He loved reading and music and was also a warrior.
- As a boy, he was "encouraged" to be a "mama's boy," a condition not helped by shyness and bad vision. In his prime, he was jaunty, healthy, athletic, and he dressed well.
- Well into his adulthood (he was thirty-five when he married Bess, whom he first met when he was eight and she was five), he formed a strong marriage and family, and a stable and unpretentious personal life.
- He was a man of regular habits (which, in the White House in those very different times, included a shot of bourbon after morning exercise and a rubdown before breakfast).
- After a difficult childhood (poverty and thwarted dreams), he came to know himself and be comfortable in his own skin.
- A man of deep but not overt faith, he had a strong moral sense that encompassed all situations, public and private.
- He was plainspoken and forthright, saying pretty much what he meant and meaning what he said.
- His work and then political life in Missouri (he held odd jobs, and was also a farmer, a soldier and a judge) and in Washington D.C. (a decade as a Senator) entailed many years of weighing conflicting courses of action aimed at doing the right thing.
- He was popular and collegial, with many "buddies" as well as close friends and intimates. Not all of these people had unblemished characters, shall I say, but somehow their mud did not stick to him.

I say all this (and could say more) to show that Truman was not a saint and that things did not come easily to him. In fact, the circumstances of his early life were enough to kill many a future, and as an adult, he did not win every battle. But I think his ground must have been exceptionally fertile when it came to making the key decision of his and millions of other people's lives.

Look at the points cited here. How many apply to you? What could you add?

By all accounts, including Truman's own, he was good at making decisions. And he had developed a philosophy for doing so that involved taking in all available information and seeking appropriate advice.

This point about philosophy is so important that I will turn to what Truman himself wrote about decision-making in his book *Where the Buck Stops*. He was referring specifically to presidential decision-making, but see if his advice is pertinent to you. It has always seemed right to me.

> The ability to make up your mind sounds as if it speaks for itself, but it really isn't as simple as all that. First of all, the president has got to get all the information he possibly can as to what's best for the most people in the Country, and that takes both basic character and self-education. He's not only got to decide what's right according to the principles by which he's been raised and educated, but he also has to be willing to listen to a lot of people, all kinds of people, and find out what effect the decision he's about to make will have on the people. And when he makes up his mind that his decision is correct, he mustn't let himself be moved from that decision under any consideration. He must go through with that program and not be swayed by the pressures that are put on him by people who tell him that his decision is wrong. If the decision is wrong, all he has to do is get some more information and make another decision, because he's also got to have the ability to change his mind and start over.

Looking back at 1945 from the vantage point of more than seventy-five years, it sometimes seems that Truman's decision to actually use the bomb and thereby end World War II, came out of the blue. But there was a lot of background.

The bomb's technology was steeped in many years of development by Allies and Americans, development that was targeted to use in the military, not in any peacetime setting such as power generation. The situation in the Pacific theater of war, always horrific, was rapidly becoming even more so—and options had run out. It was almost a given among Truman's world leadership peers that the terrible weapon would be used. In some ways, it was a fait accompli.

But as the weapon was essentially viewed as US property, only the American president's finger was on the trigger. One man's finger. Only Truman had the "nuclear codes."

When the time came to face the decision of using the atomic bomb, Truman had plenty of resources at hand. His philosophy. His character. A cohort of advisors. Reality.

But still . . .

I cannot help but think how lonely and frightened Truman must have felt at this time. Though obviously not on the same scale, I think you and I can relate. I have faced significant decisions in my life, as have you. At some point, no matter how much help is available, it falls to you and you alone.

By most accounts, the tipping point for Truman was that he could not stomach the human cost of not ending the war as soon as possible. Yes, the Japanese were on the run; they were probably just months from being defeated. But Truman's military advisors estimated that the casualties from continuing to follow the Japanese from small island to small island in the Pacific and ultimately to the large home islands—continuing to allow the enemy to set the pace and draw the Allies along—would have doubled the number of deaths and injuries that had already been suffered in the entire war effort. Brutal mathematics, with human lives the digits.

It was immediately apparent that the bomb's toll had been

even more gruesome than had been imagined. That led to public second-guessing that persists to this day. Even as more nations develop nuclear capabilities that aren't entirely military, the fact remains that a very small number of nations possess the ability to unleash "the" bomb in its full destruction. Two of those nations, as we know, are the United States and North Korea.

So far in this book, I have emphasized that Truman had and took full responsibility for the atomic bomb decision. But he did not work in a vacuum. In his toolbox was his group of advisers, both informal and official. You and I have this same tool.

Truman had many people happy to tell him what to do. He smoked cigars and often played cards with them late at night. And some of these people would have been trusted friends of long association from his personal life and his decade in the Senate. We all have such people in our lives.

Incidentally, informal groups like Truman's have come to be called the "kitchen cabinet." Now a familiar colloquialism, the term was first used to attack President Andrew Jackson's "ginger group," another great colloquialism. Jackson had purged the official Cabinet, thus called the "parlor cabinet," in 1831 during a scandal known as the Eaton affair or the petticoat affair; for information on that, well, as Casey Stengel often said, "you could look it up." Some things don't change.

And what about Bess, his wife, whom Truman called his closest political adviser, "the Boss"? In fact, she knew nothing of the bomb, and was "very angry" and "deeply disturbed" when she, like most of the rest of the world, found out about its deployment. Again, very relatable.

When he was sworn in on April 12, 1945, Truman of course inherited what I would call his "official" advisers—Cabinet members from the Roosevelt administration, and generals who were conducting the war. His trusted colleagues from his decade in the Senate did not disappear. He had peers on the world stage, the other Allied leaders Churchill and Stalin. And he had his generals—George Patton, Douglas McArthur, and others—most of whom had no reluctance to offer their views.

When you think about it, you and I have plenty of such "official" advisors, too. That said, you and I need to be careful. Truman gauged the interests and intent and motivation of his "advisors." Advice was not always offered with best thinking. You and I need to understand this, too.

In Truman's new role, it probably took a while for genuine personal and political trust to develop, but he seemed to know that these people knew more than he did. He was not going to derail the process into which he had abruptly been thrust. And certainly, he was keenly aware of the need for national stability at a time of great trauma; *The New York Times* story announcing Roosevelt's death noted that "Mr. Truman immediately let it be known that Mr. Roosevelt's Cabinet is remaining in office at his request." (It was not until 1946 that he made his own first Cabinet appointment.)

The Presidency and politics—and business, too, where I have spent my whole career—are areas of life where you can meet someone once, shake hands, communicate through interpreters if necessary and then pronounce each other "my very good friend."

How superficial!

This recalls my earlier point about Truman being in a lonely position. I think he had to depend a lot on his own sense of judgment, which was both innate and well-honed.

Consider that Truman had been vice president for five months. He was president for barely four months when he made the bomb decision. He is not known to have been present at any of the meetings among FDR, Stalin, and Churchill, and there was only one face-to-face among Truman, Stalin and Churchill. Presumably there were secure cables, telegrams, and phone calls for these world war leaders, but the age of instantaneous communication that you and I take for granted today was not even a glimmer on the horizon.

Truman seems to have been very cagey regarding Stalin. It was no secret that the U.S, was rapidly developing a useable atomic bomb. But Truman did not explicitly acknowledge this to Stalin, and Stalin apparently made the judgment the Americans would do what they needed to do to address Japan.

Churchill minced no words about the use of the atomic bomb. Referring to the July 4 meeting among the war leaders, he later wrote:

> British consent in principle to the use of the weapon had been given . . . The final decision now lay in the main with President Truman, who had the weapon; but I never doubted what it would be, nor have I ever doubted since that he was right. There was unanimous, automatic, unquestioned agreement around our table; nor did I ever hear the slightest suggestion that we should do otherwise.

That meeting, Churchill's first with Truman, may have also been their last official communication. The Conservative party lost the general election on July 5 and Churchill was therefore no longer prime minister. (All this in spite of the fact, which I have always found very curious, of the German surrender on May 7, a success that Churchill could lay some fair claim to. But other issues were obviously the deciding factor.)

As for Truman, he did not look back: "All my life, whenever it comes to me to make a decision, I make it and forget about it . . . That's all you can do."

Truman guided the United States through many other turn-

ing points in the seven years of his public life as President. The
surrender of Germany. Potsdam. The surrender of Japan. The
Truman Doctrine. The Marshall Plan. The Cold War. Com-
munism. The Civil Rights movement, including the deseg-
regation of the armed forces. The National Security Act. The
creation of Israel. The West Berlin blockade. The Fair Deal.
Korea. MacArthur. (And much more!)

Here are the top lessons I take from Truman's decision-
making process.

1. It is essential to have your own "code," made up
of your life experience, your education, your conscience,
and all the other building blocks of character. Often this
is called having a "moral compass."

2. Courage in making big decisions is not easy,
and you will get plenty of "advice." Stick to your
convictions. Have courage.

3. Try to have as many of the facts at hand as
possible. Avoid taking shots in the dark.

4. Have a group of trusted advisors already at hand—
family, friends, colleagues—and do not be afraid to
reach beyond that close circle to bring in experts as
appropriate. Consult these people! Always gauge their
motivation. And then test their advice against your
judgment.

5. Make the decision when it needs to be made.
Life moves a lot more quickly and is a lot more
interconnected than in 1945, and those factors can
pressure us to follow someone else's schedule. Do not be
impatient and rush the decision, yet do not dither. Carpe
diem in the best sense of that aphorism—move when
you need to move.

6. When you make the decision, make it. Don't be
half-hearted. Stick with it. Dedicate all the resources
needed to make it a success. Don't second-guess.

7. Always draw a conclusion—what did your decision mean? Is there more to be done?

I find so much to learn from Truman's situation in 1945. Even though you may feel alone in a decision, you are probably not. In fact, how do you call upon others when you are making a decision? And by extension, what do you do when someone calls on you?

As for others, I would say, involve them—do not rely on them. (The exception is within the family. I'll talk about that separately.) Thus:

1. Think about the people who are already good advisers to you and the level of intimacy between you. Be clear about your relationship with them.

2. Reach out to experts, framing your questions carefully. If you don't know a certain expert, you may be able to find an intermediary to introduce you—or you could just write a nice letter introducing yourself. I, myself, would respond to such a letter.

3. Know what others' qualifications are to advise you and also how much "skin they have in the game"— what's in it for them if you decide one way or the other.

4. Weigh what they say against what others say, and against your own knowledge.

5. Do not take or appear to take their advice simply to please them.

6. Research and read as much as you can about the matters you are dealing with.

And when the shoe is on the other foot and you are called upon to help someone make a decision:

1. Try to help the other person find out what he or she really wants, deep down. This is called "discernment," getting to the heart of the matter.

2. Be clear about your ability to address the question, and about your own prejudices—what's in it for you.

3. Listen actively, do not be running your own script in your head, do not pre-judge.

4. Let the decider decide. Just because you were asked, does not mean you have the responsibility for the decision. Respect the boundaries between you.

The concepts of "responsibility" and "boundaries" bring me to a very sensitive area: the decisions that take place between spouses or partners, and in the family, involving children. I will tread carefully here.

As much as I admire Truman, it is well known that he ignored Bess's wishes at a crucial time—when he first entered local politics. That disturbs me, as does Bess's reaction. Having actively advised against the decision, she continued to resent politics up to and into the White House years. Their daughter summed up the quandary this way: "Bess never hesitated to try to influence Harry Truman's decisions. But she never attempted to control him." I would add, the line between "influence" and "control" is a fine one!

I'm no marriage counselor or family therapist, but I offer this for your consideration:

1. If you have a spouse, a partner, or an adult child and are facing an important decision, do not leave these people out of your deliberations. If you do not take their advice, explain why. This is called "respect."

2. If young children are involved, certainly there are some decisions that you, as a parent, just make. No discussion! But remember that you are also responsible for teaching, guiding, assisting, and advising them when it comes to their own decisions. The balance among these actions will change as the children become adults. I think that's the point of this comment attributed to Truman, who was known as a doting father and grandfather: "I have found the best way to give advice to your children is to find out what they want and then advise them to do it."

To conclude on a light note. Was Truman destined to be plainspoken and, unlike his parents, decisive? After all, they named him Harry not Harold or Harrison, and that middle initial was just a letter (no punctuation) and didn't stand for an extra name. It stood for two names—Harry's parents couldn't decide which relative whose name began with S to honor, so they just took the letter.

2

PABLO PICASSO

> When I was a child, my mother said to me, "If you
> become a soldier, you'll be a general. If you become
> a monk, you'll end up as the Pope." Instead, I
> became a painter and wound up as Picasso.
> —PABLO PICASSO

THIS PAINTER WHO DECIDED to become Picasso created, it is
estimated, more than 20,000 works of art (or maybe almost
five times that number, depending on sourcing) in his nearly
nine-decade career. He was a complex and challenging man,
and his art was too—his paintings and drawings, his collages,
his sculptures, his graphics, his ceramics, his tapestries and his
rugs, even his poetry and his designs for the stage. Almost everything Picasso did changed the world, for he changed art.
His world-changing and enduring accomplishment, and the
focus of this chapter, is the anti-war masterpiece "Guernica,"
which he decided to paint in May 1937 in a frenzy of anger.

The delegation of Spanish politicians and personages came to
call on their countryman Pablo Picasso in his Paris studio early
in January 1937. The fifty-six-year-old artist had not lived in
Spain since 1904, and would never again in his very long life.
Yet he retained his Spanish citizenship and, more important,
his vivid and deep Spanish identity. This is what the delegation
was counting on.

The visit took place against the backdrop of the worst kind
of conflict back home. The Spanish Civil War—known in
Spain as "The War," as if there could be no other—had begun

in July 1936. Rebel Nationalist forces, under the command of Generalissimo Francisco Franco, had sought to overthrow the Republican government, which had been formed in 1931 after the intense internal strife that followed the Great War, World War I (in which Spain was officially neutral).

At the time of the politicians' visit to Picasso, both sides of the conflict had suffered bloody victories and defeats. On the one hand, Madrid lay under seemingly permanent siege by the Nationalists who were unable to break the Republicans' hold on the national capital, located in the heart of Spain. On the other hand, the Nationalists had scored with their rout of the key city of Malaga (Picasso's birthplace) in the southern part of the country. The next battlefront was shaping up along the Bay of Biscay in the north.

At the same time, the government had agreed to take part in a long-planned high-profile event, and wanted Picasso's help. Scheduled to open in Paris in May, the "1937 Paris International Exposition" was designed to showcase "art and technology in modern life." From the Republicans' point of view, Spain could use the event "as a way of revealing General Franco's cruelty to the rest of the world against a backdrop of rising authoritarianism," according to the BBC. Would Picasso, the most famous artist in the world, paint a mural for the Spanish pavilion at the Exposition?

This was not a decision Picasso wanted to make. Obviously, given the turmoil not only in Spain but in all of Europe, the Exposition would be an intense event. Hitler, Mussolini, and Stalin were spreading terror, including playing key roles in the internal Spanish strife. Countries would use the Exposition as a proxy for their conflicts with each other, their sought-after dominance and so on. While Picasso loved the country of his birth and had strong and well-known Republican leanings, he had long eschewed any overt involvement in politics. He saw little reason to change now.

There was also his personal state to consider. Turmoil and

conflict existed on the home front too. Picasso had a wife and a child, he had another child with his mistress, and he had a new mistress. Simultaneously. Perhaps this was not the time for a major new project.

Additionally, as an artist of great independence, he did not want to take on a commission. In fact, he had already offered some of his work to the Exposition, thinking it was a good venue for visibility, even though he was already legendary. Why was it his problem that the Spanish pavilion needed some panache? It was small and modest compared with the nearby German and Russian edifices that dominated the entire venue, but so what? In any event, the clock would soon start ticking, as the mural would need to be delivered in just a few months, hardly enough time for oil paint to dry.

And yet . . . was that patriotism that Picasso heard calling?

It seems that Picasso listened to the delegation and sort of said no, sort of said yes. The seed of a real decision had been planted. But he was not yet ready to act (or to paint). When he was ready, there was no yes–no back-and-forth. He would know what he needed to do. And the decision he made would change the world, because it resulted in "Guernica," the work of art that is the greatest image of anti-war defiance ever.

Gijs van Hensbergen wrote in his "biography" of the painting, "it is a powerful cry against repression while symbolizing an overwhelming desire for peace . . . Its rejection of human barbarity and its cry for liberty and peace remain as insistent today as the day Picasso put down his brush in 1937."

Picasso's situation seems familiar to me, and it must to you, too. Not because of the numerous wives and mistresses (there were eight of them in the artist's life), but because we have all equivocated when we haven't wanted to give a definite answer or make a decision. Have you ever smilingly taken part in a meeting and given the impression that you were "on board," only to resolve the moment you left the meeting, "no way"?

Have you ever felt persuaded in one direction when talking to one person, only to change your stance when talking to another person?

Equivocation is not an attractive quality, but it is a human one. It allows us to avoid difficult dilemmas. It can serve a protective function, too, if it causes us to hit the pause button and take time to make a decision.

What brought Picasso to this point of decision in his life? Let's take a quick look.

He seemed born—on October 25, 1881, in Malaga, Spain—to be an artist. His father was an artist, a professor of art and a museum curator at various times in his life. According to his mother, young Pablo drew before he could talk, and his first word was "piz-piz," baby-talk for "lápiz" or "pencil."

His classical art tutelage began under his father. As sometimes happens, the student surpassed the teacher. In Pablo's case, he was thirteen when his father himself stopped painting, in recognition of his son's talent, and gave his own supplies to his son. Formal study took place starting at age ten at the School of Fine Arts in La Coruna, where his father taught. Then followed the School of Fine Arts in Barcelona (starting at age thirteen) and the prestigious Royal Academy of San Fernando in Madrid (at age sixteen). Picasso chafed at the Royal Academy's formal requirements and seldom attended classes, preferring to spend his time at the Prado Museum.

"Because of his academic training, (his father) believed training consisted of copying of masterworks and drawing the human figure from live-figure models and plaster casts," according to the Pablo Picasso website. This kind of training endures today, because many people believe that it imparts a strong foundation to any artist.

Already prolific and highly inventive, and beginning to move beyond his classical roots, Picasso moved to Paris in 1904. There he began the career and the life that would be uniquely his, that would make him "Picasso," the man his Spanish visitors would call on thirty-three years later. He died on April 8, 1973, in his ninety-second year, never having stopped creating art.

Picasso was so productive, so versatile, so inventive and explorative over so many years, that his output is classified in "periods." He seemed to make decided changes at chronological markers as he "exhausted" one style, palette, or approach, and began another:

Blue (melancholy palette and mood): 1901–1904

Rose (happy palette and mood): 1904–1906

African-Art-Influenced/Primitivism: 1907–1909

Cubism: 1909–1912

(So-called) Return to Order (synthesis): 1914–1919

Neoclassicism and Surrealism: 1918–1945

Late/Final: 1945–1973

Into the spring of 1937, the Nationalist and the Republican forces continued their tragic battles on their own Spanish homeland. The war front had moved north, along the Bay of Biscay. The northeastern part of this area, right at the French border, nestled remotely in the Pyrenees Mountains, was, and still is, the beautiful, fertile and traditional center of life for the Basque people. The Basques are a unique indigenous group with their own language, customs, and ethnic connections. "Basque Country" is, to this day, neither Spanish nor French, yet both. Guernica ("Gernika" in the Basque language) was a typical Basque village, population about 7,000.

And Guernica was where, on April 26, 1937, a horrible wartime tragedy took place. Aimed at civilians, it was no accident. Under the code name "Operation Rügen," German and Italian aircraft, working to support the Nationalists, attacked the village and destroyed it. Guernica was bombed, strafed, exploded, and burnt into oblivion. There has never been a full accounting of the number of deaths. Depending on which sources you consult, estimates have ranged from the low hundreds to well into the thousands. Just outside the village, a munitions factory and a communications center were left untouched, so it was clear who and what Operation Rügen's target was—innocent civilians.

The attack had "no strategic military significance," noted an analysis many years later. Still, the door was now open for the Nationalist forces to capture the port city of Bilbao, the Basque's largest, and the rest of northern Spain. "The War" would continue until 1939, with Hitler and Mussolini behind the Nationalists, and Stalin behind the Republicans. And then would commence World War II.

News traveled more slowly in 1937 than it does now. World-renowned war correspondent George Steer was on-site and immediately issued the very first reports on the atrocity: "The Tragedy of Guernica/Town Destroyed in Air Attack/Eye-Witness's Account" read the next day's headline in *The Times* of London. Even with news of the outrage spreading throughout the world's newspapers and radios, it was several days before the full import of the attack on Guernica would begin to be recognized. In Paris, Picasso would probably have seen the first terrible photographs on May 1 and read stories with blaring headlines such as "VISIONS DE GUERNICA EN FLAMMES."

And Picasso made his decision. This was "the instant Picasso knew what would be the subject of his mural for the exhibition," as art historian Fernando Martin Martin (yes, that's his name) said, adding: "For the first time in the contemporary history of war, a town and its civilian population had been annihilated both as a scare tactic and as a way of testing the war machine."

Even though he was a permanent expatriate, Picasso was still a son of Spain, and he was angry. He would paint a mural for the Spanish pavilion. He knew exactly what its subject would be. No, not a huge depiction of an artist at the easel (himself, of course; he did have an ego), which was one of the ideas be had been playing with. He would show what war really looked like. He would paint "Guernica" . . . "a painting that will be as powerful as his fury," as Alain Serres wrote.

Here is another aspect of decision-making to consider. When you make a decision, do you want to put it into action immediately? Some decisions are like that! Certainly, decisions made in emergencies define timeliness. Others, once made, can continue to ripen. I'm not advocating anything here, just asking you to take note.

In the months between January and April/May 1937, what was Picasso doing besides stewing over this decision? Largely, he was creating a series of satiric etchings called "Dream and Lie of Franco." The etchings contained panels of cartoonish, profane and vulgar depictions of the rebellious leader, along with many tortured-looking creatures and people. The printed etchings were supposed to be cut into individual panels, like baseball cards or playing cards. The idea was that these would be distributed casually throughout the public to raise awareness and, yes, anger. All this honed Picasso's own simmering anger of what was happening to Spain. Many drawings were also produced in the early months of that year that clearly foreshadow the imagery that would appear in Guernica.

Have you ever made decisions when you were very angry or otherwise very emotional? Know that I have, and they were not among my best. But I have done "prep work" for decisions while I have been angry. You could call these "cooling-off periods." They have helped me to discharge negative energy and to formulate my plans going forward.

Picasso was not the first artist to depict war and its aftermath. As is now known, Spain contains very early evidence of art. Dating from 30,000 years ago, some 700 sites are in caves of the eastern-most portion of the Iberian Peninsula. On the rock walls of these caves are many tiny images of stick-figure humans, and many of these images are . . . throwing spears and using bow-and-arrow weapons.

And let's not forget that Picasso lived through World War I. As a thirty-something expatriate citizen of a neutral country, he himself did not see battle. But many of his friends did, some mortally, and as an artist, he responded to their experiences and what he observed living in battle-torn France. Or even traveling to the front himself. Many powerful paintings exist from this time.

As a classically trained artist, Picasso would also have been familiar with many battlefield paintings. Think of Rubens' "Consequences of War" (1638–39) or Copley's "The Death of Major Peirson" (1783) or Goya's "The Third of May, 1808" (1814) or Sargent's "Gassed" (1919). Was he also aware of Mathew Brady's Civil War photography? Even so, these works, and there are many more, generally feature warfare's effects on its military participants. Picasso's aim was to show its effects on civilians, the innocent citizens who are often cited by leaders as the reasons war is waged in the first place.

Knowing that Picasso knew all his art antecedents helps us appreciate that he did not imitate the scrawls of a child (as some critics said about his work from 1904 on and during his life; few do now). He was inventing new visual languages. Languages are available to all who care to learn them. Robert Rauschenberg, for one, said that studying the composition of the "Guernica" helped him develop the abstract fluency that characterized his own ground-breaking paintings. (Jasper Johns said that Rauschenberg "invented the most since Picasso.")

Maybe this phenomenon is why Picasso supposedly said, "Bad artists copy. Good artists steal." Can Picasso's observation be expanded to other fields? In your own world, does copying and stealing happen? I don't mean in the sense of literally taking someone else's work and claiming it as your own, but in the sense that there is a reservoir of knowledge we can all drink from. The "canon" should be available to all. It helps us make decisions.

Picasso's art education, and his own preferences, attracted him greatly to the use of symbols in art. In "Consequences of War," Rubens presents the European Thirty Years' War as an allegory, with Mars, Venus, and various cherubs among the protagonists. In "Guernica," Picasso presents a heart-wrenching allegory based on a selection of his own personal symbols. For many years, he had been developing and employing these symbols, which sometimes had conflicting meanings, depending on how he used them. Some were based on myths and religion, psychology and eroticism, others on childhood memories. Many were also infused with Spanish nationality. I daresay that countless academic theses have been written analyzing the rich symbolism of the images of "Guernica" and how Picasso's decision to rely on them helped assure the painting's greatness.

Symbols can be universal, and they can be so personal or arcane that no one else knows what they mean. They can also be shortcuts to communication. Families, for example, often have symbols the mere mention of which causes knowing laughter—no more explanation needed. Do you have, or use, symbols?

Symbols depicted in "Guernica" include the horse, the bull/minotaur, the dove, the mother/child, the lone woman, the lamp, the light bulb; natural and architectural elements are also present.

The color palette of "Guernica" represents another area of artistic decision-making. From his Blue and his Rose periods, we know that Picasso knew how to use color to denote mood. Prior to the Spanish war, his work was characterized by abundant color. With his deliberate decision to use only white, muted blacks and grays and a little blue, Picasso showed us how he wanted us to feel.

After "Guernica" was finished, he largely returned to a vibrant palette, though there was a major exception: "The Charnel House," painted in 1944–45. Clearly, Picasso was still defying war. I'll quote directly from the website of the Museum of Modern Art in New York:

> Echoing "Guernica" in its composition, abstracted
> forms and political content, "The Charnel House"
> was inspired by newspaper war photographs, the tones
> of which are reflected in its somber black-and-white
> palette. While "Guernica," a commentary on the
> Spanish Civil War, may be seen as signaling the violent
> beginning of World War II, "The Charnel House"
> marks its horrific end.

My wife, Jan, is an artist, and for many years I have been a privileged witness to her creative process, which can be described as a cascade of decisions. Often what comes first is an overall but not-yet-directed sense of inspiration. Then comes the idea, sometimes immediately and sometimes after long germination. Then there is a consideration of choices about what to do with and about the idea. Will it be painted in oil or acrylic? How large will it be? Will it be a single painting or part of an inter-related series? As she works to bring her idea to life, changes take place. Maybe she adjusts the composition or the color palette, maybe she scrapes everything off the canvas and starts over.

So too with the "Guernica." "I begin with an idea and it becomes something else," said Picasso, who also said, "Inspiration exists, but it has to find you working."

Once his "big" decision had been made, a stream of smaller decisions followed, seemingly in rapid-fire succession. Sketches of the various images, composition of the images, considerations of color choices, preliminary studies—all these elements and more whirled about, subject to Picasso's powerful creative desire to express the horror of a specific bombing that was to become a lasting depiction of the horror of all war.

After about a month of constant work (documented photographically by his new mistress Dora Maar), Picasso declared that the enormous oil painting (canvas stretched over an 11'6" x 25'6" frame) was finished. It was installed at the Spanish pavilion in early June 1937, and its public life began.

There is a story that when a German general saw "Guernica," he said to Picasso, who was standing nearby, "Did you do this?" Picasso answered, "No, you did." (A few years later, during the Nazi occupation of France, 1940–44, Picasso's work would be considered "degenerate," forbidden to be shown in public.)

After the Exposition ended, "Guernica" began touring the world to continue to keep the plight of Spain front-and-center. After the end of the war, Picasso sold the painting to the government, despite the proviso that it would never be displayed in Spain during Franco's lifetime.

Eventually, the ever more fragile painting was shipped to the Museum of Modern Art in New York. It remained there on permanent display until it was transferred to Spain on September 10, 1981, the centenary of its creator's birth. (Franco had died in 1975, but various disputes had delayed the eventual transfer to Spain.) Prior to the opening of the Museo Bilbao Guggenheim in 1997, there was a tentative plan to install "Guernica" in that museum for obvious reasons, but the plan never came to fruition. The masterwork lives now in the Museo Reina Sofia in Madrid, protected by glass and guards.

Despite the painting's specific geographical title and the historical source of its inspiration, "Guernica" is universal. Therein lies its world-changing power. According to the official website of the Museo Reina Sofia (emphasis added):

> Neither the studies nor the finished picture contain a single allusion to a specific event, constituting instead *a generic plea against the barbarity and terror of war.* The huge picture is conceived as a giant poster, testimony to the horror that the Spanish Civil War was causing and a forewarning of what was to come in the Second World War. The muted colours, the intensity of each and every one of the motifs and the way they are articulated are all essential to the extreme tragedy of the scene, which would become *the emblem for all the devastating tragedies of modern society.*

You may know that, starting in 1985 (with an absence of several years for restorations), a tapestry version of "Guernica" has hung at the United Nations. A gift from Nelson Rockefeller's estate, it is located in the hallway outside the entrance to the Security Council meeting room, where TV crews often gather for press conferences. You may recall that, when Secretary of State Colin Powell came to the Security Council on February 5, 2003, to discuss invading Iraq, U.N. officials temporarily covered up the tapestry with a blue curtain and flags of nations. This was either to provide a better backdrop for the cameras—or to prevent, many thought, the grotesquery of a new war being advocated with "Guernica" as witness.

Lessons to learn from Picasso and how he lived his life?

1. Avoid equivocating. Be firm and focused.
2. Always consider the other person and the impact you will have on that individual.

3. When possible take your decision to a larger purpose.

4. Whenever possible use symbols to punctuate your point.

5. Apply your talent wisely and where you can make a difference.

6. Infuse as much creativity as possible into what you do.

3

ELIE WIESEL

As if the choice were in our own hands.
—ELIE WIESEL

This sentence appears about halfway through *Night,* Elie Wiesel's heartrending telling of his time, as a teenage Jewish boy, in Hitler's World War II death camps in Poland and Germany. At this point in this classic memoir, Elie knows that his mother and his little sister have perished, early on, in the poison gas. He knows this because he saw them being led away. His two older sisters are imprisoned somewhere, he assumes, and he and his father are suffering together in Auschwitz and then Buna Werke. But at least they are together. That is the only thing Elie can count on, can focus on.

Please remember this sentence about choice, which Elie would write sometime in the future, from a memory tinged with sarcasm or resignation or bewilderment or irony. Tragedy, for sure. Because long before the Nazis had arrived in 1944 to empty the ghettoes of Sighet (in Romania), where Elie and his family lived, it was already too late—there would be no choice for them.

About three-quarters through the book *Night*—if you can bear to read so far into this saddest of documents—comes an excruciating passage. There are so many more. . . . This one comes at a time when Elie has been hospitalized in the Buna camp after surgery without anesthesia for a grossly infected foot. He can barely walk. His father is nearby.

Rumors are swirling that Buna is to be evacuated, emptied—perhaps the Russians have broken through the eastern front—

and all the residents withdrawn to "the depths of Germany, to other camps; there was no shortage of them." Both the commandants and the prisoners seem to be frantic. It was known that the Nazis would often blow up camps after they themselves abandoned them, even if prisoners were still there. The Nazis were also apt to give orders that "all the invalids will be summarily killed" because it was efficient to "finish off the sick." But maybe not; one of the many tools the camp commandants wielded to degrade their prisoners was utter randomness.

Elie writes, "I did not want to be separated from my father. We had already suffered so much, borne so much together; this was not the time to be separated." Three times, he asks his father what they are to do. His father remains mute. The tension builds.

Writing years later, Elie recalls, "The choice was in our hands. For once we could decide our fate for ourselves. . . . Or else we could follow the others." Finally, Elie makes the decision for both of them, to "be evacuated with the others." His father answers, "Let's hope we shan't regret it, Eliezer."

In this brief moment, did the teenage boy and his father make the "right" decision?

Elie's words take my breath away:

> I learned after the war the fate of those who had
> stayed behind in the hospital. They were quite simply
> liberated by the Russians two days after the evacuation.

Elie and his father, along with so many others, are force-marched to "the depths of Germany," to Buchenwald. Some short time later, Elie's father is dead, but not before begging his son for a drink of water that never comes, and Elie—well, here are his words again:

> I have nothing to say of my life during this period.
> It no longer mattered. After my father's death, nothing
> could touch me anymore.

You are reading a book about world-changing decisions
and the people who made them. Did this single concentration
camp decision change the world? Certainly for Elie Wiesel
and his father it did—it changed the small world as they knew
it. Along the way, other decisions—ones that they made and
ones that were forced upon them—had already changed the
world for the Wiesel family and their neighbors in the ghetto
of Sighet. But were these true decisions, made with freedom
of choice?

Wiesel grapples with the concept of freedom as he reacts—
or more precisely, does not—to his father's death:

> I did not weep, and it pained me that I could not
> weep. But I had no more tears. And in the depths of my
> being, in the recesses of my weakened conscience, could
> I have searched it, I might perhaps have found something
> like—free at last.

Wiesel's conscience is in such disrepair because, heartbreakingly, in the depths of his own pain and degradation under the
Nazis, he has begun to forget about his father. Shortly before
his father's death:

> It was daytime when I awoke. And then I
> remembered that I had a father . . . I had known that
> he was at the end, on the brink of death, and yet I
> had abandoned him . . . Immediately I felt ashamed of
> myself, ashamed forever.

Are decisions made without freedom valid decisions? Are
decisions made under the most extreme of circumstances—
death or its near certainty—valid? Or are they the purest of
decisions?

My thoughts turn to the late Senator John McCain. We
all know his biography. A thirty-one-year-old Navy fighter
pilot in the Vietnam War, he was shot out of the sky in 1967

and fell to earth with grievous injuries, many broken bones. Captured, he received little to no medical aid but constant torture designed to break him. His captors offered him early release—"freedom"—because of who his father was: Admiral Jack McCain, commander-in-chief of the Pacific Command as of 1968. Airman McCain, from his own sense of honor and his awareness of his value as a piece of propaganda, made the decision to say "No." This led to years more imprisonment and torture, including beatings and long periods of solitary confinement. He was a prisoner of war for more than five years.

At some point, the torture did succeed in breaking him. He was forced to recite and record an enemy-supplied false statement condemning the United States and praising his captors. I think this qualifies as the most extreme of circumstances, don't you? Had John McCain made a decision? Or was he no longer capable of the agency—the freedom—needed to make a real decision?

For Senator McCain, this experience led to at least two decisions he lived with for the rest of his life. First, he openly admitted that he had "confessed"; though deeply ashamed, as was Elie Wiesel by his actions, like Elie he never flinched. As he said, "Every man has his breaking point." Second, McCain never ceased to express his abhorrence of torture. He opposed its use by any country, but especially the United States. Pragmatically, he believed that it produced only faulty intelligence, nothing useful. Most vitally, he called torture "immoral."

Thank God most of us have never been in such an extreme circumstance.

I have made many difficult and complicated decisions in my career. Like many, I have made decisions when faced with adverse health situations or helped family members do the same. I have made many thoughtful and joyful decisions; most important, to persuade my wife that we should be married. Jointly, my wife and I have made many thoughtful and joyful decisions;

most important, to have our children. We made the delightful decisions of naming our sons. And we have made many practical and fun decisions over the years—where to live, where to go on vacation, and what to have for dinner.

None of these decisions were in extremis. As is probably the case with you, they all pale in comparison with the decisions faced such men as Elie Wiesel and John McCain. Or by the few remaining members of the Donner Party who resorted to cannibalism as they starved in the Sierra Nevada Mountains on the way to California in the brutal winter of 1846–47. The people in the Twin Towers who, with the absolute certainty of death before them on that pristine morning in September 2001, jumped—or didn't. The cancer sufferer—maybe your own family member or friend—who considers stopping all treatment. Or the adult child who has been entrusted with health care power of attorney over an elderly, terminally ill parent with dementia. Or the family called to the ER after a car accident renders their teen brain-injured and comatose.

Recently, it was recommended that I read a book called *Einstein and the Rabbi,* by Naomi Levy. The book is about a rabbi, Robert Marcus, who could not recover from crippling grief over the death of his young son. Rabbi Marcus sought answers on life's meaning from Albert Einstein, whom he didn't know. This happened in the early '50s, when Rabbi Marcus was still immersed in his life's work. This work entailed rescuing Jewish children from the death camps after the end of World War II and bringing them the restoration needed to get on with their lives, if possible. The book's author is herself a rabbi and wrote her book in 2017 as part of her long process of seeking healing from the death of her beloved father many years earlier. When she comes upon the story of the rabbi and Einstein, she decides to follow it up.

In her research, Rabbi Levy learns that one of Rabbi Marcus's young rescues had been a teenager who sat in the corner and wrote and wrote and wrote. Turns out this boy was Elie Wiesel. What he was writing would become *Night*.

(Einstein counseled Rabbi Marcus on the oneness of the universe, and therefore of life. And that's the counsel that helped Rabbi Levy, too.)

What Elie Wiesel and his family and six million others were swept up in, of course, was the Holocaust. The teenager writing in the corner became the adult who dedicated his life to the clarion call of "never again." Even so, genocide, ethnic cleansing—whatever horrible names are used—are decisions by governments and other entities that persist and even flourish in our time. And there are some people, I shudder to write, who openly deny that the Holocaust ever took place.

Eliezer Wiesel was born in September 1928. He would later say that his father Shlomo gave him Jewish scholarship and his mother Sarah gave him Jewish faith—head and heart-soul, I would say. Elie's imprisonment began in May 1944 when he was still fifteen; he was liberated from Buchenwald by American forces in the spring of 1945. The Nazis had been defeated, and eventually he was reunited with his two sisters. Within months, in September 1945, Japan surrendered and World War II was over. Millions of people had to learn how to live again.

Wiesel began the process by obtaining his education at the Sorbonne and becoming a journalist and writer of books, encouraged by the Catholic novelist and thinker François Mauriac. *Night* was published in French in 1956 and in English in 1960. At first, no one knew what to make of *Night*—was it autobiography, fiction, fantasy, art? It was certainly unique. Gradually, as knowledge of the actuality of the Holocaust took hold, the book's power as a memoir became overwhelming. Best estimates are that more than ten million copies have been sold, in over thirty countries.

Wiesel's next two books were *Dawn* and *Day,* forming a trilogy with *Night*. Though highly informed by his concentration camp experiences, *Dawn* and *Day* were decidedly novels. Over the years, Wiesel would write nearly sixty books of many genres. After he moved to New York City in 1955 and became an American citizen, he married in 1969 and became a father in 1972. He also became a professor and a global peace and Jewish faith activist.

Wiesel never feared "speaking truth to power." In April 1985, he was awarded the Congressional Gold Medal of Achievement, the nation's highest civilian honor, by President Ronald Reagan. At the ceremony, which Wiesel had threatened to boycott, Wiesel publicly criticized the president for planning to lay a wreath at the Bitburg cemetery for Nazi war dead during the upcoming presidential trip to Germany.

Speaking about Bitburg, Wiesel voiced the outrage of many when he said to Reagan:

> May I, Mr. President, if it's possible at all, implore you to do something else, to find a way, to find another way, another site? That place, Mr. President, is not your place. Your place is with the victims of the SS.

The trip was also to include a visit to the Bergen-Belsen concentration camp where Anne Frank died. According to *The New York Times,* Reagan "stared unflinching" at Wiesel and, though apparently moved, "left quickly." The trip went on as planned.

The next year, 1986, Elie Wiesel won the Nobel Peace Prize. The Nobel Committee's citation noted his "practical work in the cause of peace, atonement and human dignity." In 2009, Wiesel would accompany President Barack Obama for a somber tour of Buchenwald during a European trip to commemorate D-Day. In the official U.S. statement after Wiesel's death, Obama hailed him as "one of the great moral voices of his time, and in many ways, the conscience of the world."

I was privileged to know Elie Wiesel. We first met in 1993, when he was based in New York and I was newly arrived from Chicago. He was actively traveling the world on his self-designed mission to make sure no one forgot the Holocaust or ignored the many ongoing examples of genocide. His wife Marion (who had a different sort of wartime survival story from her childhood in Vichy, France) did the same, either with him or in connection with her own humanitarian work.

Wiesel was a serious and engaging man. One knew he was a person of good caliber who was intent on his goal.

In late 2008, the gigantic financial swindle perpetrated by Bernie Madoff was exposed. Among the thousands of victims was Elie Wiesel. Every single dollar invested with Madoff was lost; in Wiesel's case, amounting to about $15 million from his foundation and an additional large amount personally. The overall Madoff swindle topped $65 billion.

I went to call on Wiesel. We discussed how he could possibly recover from his bad decision to put all his financial eggs in the Madoff basket. Together with other like-minded people, we devised a plan that, thanks to donors large and small, named and unnamed, replaced Wiesel's losses dollar-for-dollar. This generosity enabled Wiesel to continue his work for another eight years, until he died.

In interviews after the Madoff debacle, Wiesel spoke of forgiveness, which he decidedly did not offer. Quoted by CNN, he said, almost brazenly:

> Could I forgive him? No. To forgive, first of all, would mean that he would come on his knees and ask for forgiveness. He wouldn't do that . . . It's the inhumanity in this man . . .

Wiesel did speak of a suitable punishment for Madoff in that same CNN piece:

> I would like him to be in a solitary cell with a screen, and on that screen . . . every day and every night there should be pictures of his victims, one after the other

after the other, always saying, "Look, look what you have done to this poor lady, look what you have done to this child, look what you have done" . . . he should not be able to avoid those faces, for years to come. This is only a minimum punishment.

We are all aware of the "crisis" at our southern border because of the U.S. government's decision to separate thousands of children from their parents and families. These children have been housed in detention facilities, tent cities, camps.

Whether seeking asylum legally or breaking the law, their parents have viewed the United States as a place of safety. And yet, the same government that, in our name as Americans, liberated Hitler's camps perpetuates this growing horror. Is it not also in our name? What would Wiesel have said about this? Would he have decided to speak out?

Many people are doing so this very minute, including psychologists and social workers who realize the grave damage being done to the psyches of these little children, some of them not even schoolage. How will these children survive and thrive? Wiesel must have been exposed to the same kind of psychological damage. What caused him not to be destroyed by his death camp experiences? Surely, he was marked, but in a way that allowed him to be the "eloquent witness . . . who seared the memory of the Holocaust on the world's conscience," as Joseph Berger wrote in Wiesel's obituary in *The New York Times* on July 2, 2016.

I am reminded of another Jewish adolescent trying to grow up in the mid-'40s in Europe—the Dutch girl Anne Frank. She was born in June of 1929. As the world knows, she and her family and some friends spent two whole years, starting in the summer of 1942, hiding together in a cramped two-room attic that they called their "secret annexe." Essentially, they imprisoned themselves by their own decision not to flee from

their native city of Amsterdam as the Nazi threat of occupation loomed. In August of 1944, an act of betrayal brought the
"annexe" to the attention of the Gestapo. The intrepid group
was forced into various concentration camps. Anne was sent
to Westerbork in Holland and then to Auschwitz and Bergen-
Belsen, where she died in March of 1945 of the typhus that had
engulfed the camp. She was not quite sixteen years old.

During the time in the attic hiding place, Anne confided
in her "friend" Kitty—the name she gave to her diary—as
honestly as any teen-age girl anywhere. That ended when the
Gestapo came. After the war, her father Otto, the only survivor
of the family, found and published *The Diary of Anne Frank*.
This book gives us its own view, as surely as *Night* does, of the
innocence that was slaughtered by the Nazis—and which all
genocides, all violence, all detention have in common.

Remember young Elie and his father in their camps? The
dynamic of their relationship culminated in—let's face it as
squarely as Elie did—his betrayal of his father. When I first
encountered *Night,* I was too young to plumb its depths. Even
so, I was gripped by Elie's actions then and still am. I, too, am
a son and the father of sons. Elie saw others in the camps who,
like him, turned their backs on their elders because of the same
loss of human dignity. Were all these actions decisions? I wonder if my reaction resonates with everyone else.

I also wonder if Anne's story echoes in a similar way. In the
hothouse atmosphere of the Franks' hiding place, Anne (who
"ages" from thirteen to fifteen), was constantly at odds with
her mother and often with everyone else. (She's a teenager!)
In often florid terms, Anne confided her distress to Kitty-the-
diary. For example:

> The horrible words, mocking looks, and accusations
> which are leveled at me repeatedly every day, and find
> their mark, like shafts from a tightly strung bow, and
> which are just as hard to draw from my body.

We can almost see her eyes roll as she writes this and more. (She's a teenager!) But we know, as Anne and her mother never would, how this would end. Her father would know, though, and I think of the pain in his soul as he read his daughter's words after his family was all dead. Even so, he decided to approve their publication. Many women have told me that the never-to-be-rectified mother-daughter dynamic pervades their reading of *Diary*.

Elie Wiesel was given the gift of surviving and decided to bear full witness. In doing so, he changed the world. He started with *Night* and continued for the rest of his long life; he was eighty-seven when he died. It seems to me that he tried valiantly to overcome what he knew he had become at age seventeen. *Night* concludes:

One day I was able to get up, after gathering all my strength. I wanted to see myself in the mirror hanging on the opposite wall. I had not seen myself since the ghetto. From the depths of the mirror, a corpse gazed back at me. The look in his eyes, as they stared into mine, has never left me.

Anne Frank was not given the gift of surviving. Her tragedy is that she could not fulfill what she yearned for, as every young person does. She addressed Kitty:

I get so confused by it all that I either laugh or cry: it depends on what sort of mood I am in. Then I fall asleep with a stupid feeling of wishing to be different from what I am or from what I want to be; perhaps to behave differently from the way I want to behave or do behave. Oh, heavens above, now I am getting you in a muddle too.

Through the decision of her father, posthumously Anne and her *Diary* also bear full witness and have changed the world. "I want to go on living even after my death," she told Kitty, and surely she does.

Are there are children today, in the "tent cities" on the southern border, who will change the world because they will decide to bear witness?

Let's think about how everything I have told you in this chapter relates to my and your ability to make good decisions, day-to-day.

1. Pay attention to what is happening around you, in your own "small" life and in the larger world. Ignorance of reality cannot possibly lead to good decisions.

2. Forgive yourself if you are swept up in forces beyond your control and make bad, stupid or ineffectual decisions, even if you cannot change them. Forgive yourself even if there are no such forces. As surely as (God willing) a baby rolls over, then creeps, then crawls, and then becomes a child who walks and runs, you must always go forward. Humans are born to do that.

3. Try to forgive, or at least understand, other people who make bad decisions that affect you. If neither forgiveness nor understanding can happen, remember that we are all flawed human beings—and go forward.

4. Try to help people who are suffering the effects of their own bad decisions. Not only is this "good karma," it can help you avoid the same mistakes.

5. Keep your decisions in perspective. Many are vital, many are not. Even so, try to take all of them seriously.

6. Never give up.

4

MAHATMA GANDHI, DAG HAMMARSKJÖLD

Before an important decision, someone clutches
your hand—a glimpse of gold in the iron-gray, the
proof of all you have never dared believe.
—DAG HAMMARSKJÖLD

HAVE YOU EVER FELT that a major decision had suddenly imposed itself on you? Appearing seemingly out of nowhere, possibly propelled by outside forces, but actually the inevitable
result of your experience. In such a circumstance, it becomes
absolutely clear what you must do. I have had that clarity and
conviction in both personal and professional settings.

On the other hand . . .

Have you ever felt that a major decision had crept up on
you? That you didn't consciously set out to make a decision,
but there it was, the natural result of your experience. In such
a circumstance, the decision seems to make itself. Again, familiar to me.

One scenario seems like it might belong to Mahatma (Mohandas) Gandhi, the other to Dag Hammarskjöld. Both were
men of peace whose decisions about nonviolence changed the
world.

Let's take a look at Gandhi first.

"Out of the blue" is a way to describe what happened to
Mohandas Gandhi on the night in May 1893 when he made
the decision that would define the rest of his life and shape the

lives of tens of millions. Gandhi had just been the target of an act of racial violence that was both insulting to him and completely understandable, a natural outcome of life in stratified South Africa.

His response changed the world.

On that night in 1893, Gandhi was a twenty-four-year-old lawyer, trained in England and working in South Africa. Having had little success in practicing law in his native India, he had taken a limited-term assignment in Durban for an Indian-owned shipping firm. This is not as far-fetched as it might seem, for both countries were linked as part of the British Empire and there was significant commerce between them. Even over a century ago, the Indian population in South Africa was sizeable. (Today, South Africa has the second largest Indian population in the world.) But Indians in South Africa were considered the lowest of the low, at the bottom of all the other "nonwhite" people. Even with about 78 percent of the population being nonwhite, rampant discrimination was enforced by the roughly 22 percent that was white. Today, about 8 percent of the population is white.

That night, Ghandi was traveling by train the 300-some miles from Durban to Pretoria, with a ticket to the first-class compartment. The conductor ordered him to move to the "van" (trucks) compartment, and Gandhi knew why. A white passenger had objected to his presence. But Gandhi refused to move, observing that he had a paid ticket entitling him to be in the first-class compartment. The conductor persisted, Gandhi resisted—but the result was that the young lawyer was summarily ejected from the train onto the platform at the Pietermaritzburg station. His luggage was tossed out after him, and the train went on its way.

Gandhi spent a long, cold, lonely night huddled in the dark of the waiting room, waiting for another train. He reviewed his life and his situation. Apparently, he couldn't make a living in his home country. In his temporary adopted country of South Africa, he was in fact making a living and beginning to make a difference. But . . . he was "nonwhite," an insurmountable obstacle. "Apartheid" was not yet an official South African policy (which it was from 1948 to 1994), but in terms of daily life for close to two million people, it might as well have been.

By the time morning came, Gandhi had made his decision—he would begin to stand up to the racial prejudice that surrounded him and his fellow Indian citizens in South Africa. He would begin to hone and use a tool of nonviolent action that was new in the world of conflict—specifically, "satyagraha," passive resistance, from the Sanskrit words for "truth" and "insistence."

Indian liberation within South Africa became Gandhi's focus for the twenty-one years that he remained in that country. He returned to India in 1914 with an expanded goal: total independence of India from the British Empire. He also wanted to transform Indian society. The rest, as someone has said, is history. A history whose worldwide influence would be permanent. A history of so much opposition that it culminated in his assassination thirty-four years later by a fanatical opponent, as the "Father of India" was on his way to his usual evening public prayer event.

The Civil Rights movement in the United States contains many examples of satyagraha, a potent and not always pretty force that contains many contradictions. Satyagraha itself is not violent, it is passive. Think of Rosa Parks just not giving up her seat on that bus in Montgomery, Alabama, on December 1, 1955. That simple gesture became the centerpiece of the Montgomery Bus Boycott. But satyagraha is also resistance, meaning that there is an opposing force, and violence is often the response to the passive action. Marches, sit-ins and protest demonstrations, for example, are common forms of resistance. Think of "Bloody Sunday" on March 7, 1965 in

Selma, Alabama, when 600 people, led by Martin Luther King Jr. in a voting rights march, were viciously beaten. Or think of the controversy reflected in this *New York Times* headline from August 12, 2017: "Man Charged After White Nationalist Rally in Charlottesville Ends in Deadly Violence."

What made that train station decision world-changing is not "merely" that Gandhi's work and life ultimately led to India's independence. Rather, that Gandhi also achieved his goal of social transformation—global, in fact, not just Indian. Nonviolence took its rightful place in all aspects of life. Along the way, Gandhi acquired the honorific Indian title "Mahatma"—"great soul" or "revered."

Gandhi's familiar garb was a form of satyagraha against expensive imported manufactured textiles and part of a larger boycott of all British goods. Starting in 1921, Gandhi abandoned typical "western" men's dress and for the rest of his life, swathed himself in the traditional woven "dhoti" (loincloth) and shawl. This was a personal gesture, which he did not encourage his followers to emulate. He also devoted himself to the traditional art of spinning, so much so that the spinning wheel became a national symbol. Both actions put him in solidarity with the poor. The hunger strikes that Gandhi was known for, and that many subsequent protestors have adopted as a tool, was another form of satyagraha.

A supreme irony is that another act of violence—his assassination in 1948—ended the life of this man who came to exemplify nonviolence.

When Saul of Tarsus was struck down from his horse and made blind on the road to Damascus early in the first century A.D., the abrupt redirection of his life entered our language as a "conversion experience."

When Mohandas Gandhi was thrown off that train in Pietermaritzburg almost 2,000 years later, he had a very similar "conversion experience." In his autobiography, Gandhi wrote that is when his mission in life began: "I discovered that as a man and as an Indian, I had no rights." He also said, "All the alterations I have made in my life have been effected by momentous occasions."

Now let's turn to Hammarskjöld and his world-changing decision.

Gradual inevitability seems to characterize the Swedish diplomat Dag Hammarskjöld. In contrast to Gandhi, Hammarskjöld's decision process took place over a long period of time, as he matured in his life and his career. It culminated in his service in 1953–1961 as the second Secretary-General of the United Nations. The U.N. had been formed in 1945, as the ashes of World War II were still warm amid the still vivid memories of World War I, to help assure that there would never again be a world war. Hammarskjöld's U.N. service caused him to be hailed by JFK as "the greatest statesman of our century."

What distinguished Hammarskjöld was that he built upon the age-old traditions of diplomacy and made them relevant to the new challenges posed by a different kind of world war, the Cold War.

Diplomacy itself is a broad and over-arching philosophy of how to maintain good relations between individuals and nations. It plays out over long periods of time. Because it is strategic rather than tactical, results are only sometimes immediate or clear-cut. We may notice (and enjoy!) diplomacy's public pomp and circumstance, but there is much work behind-the-scenes that is not glamorous. Within that general framework, Hammarskjöld decided to use the targeted tactics of "quiet diplomacy" and "preventive diplomacy" to avoid or avert possible conflicts before they even came to the stage of negotiation. This kind of enhanced diplomacy is almost entirely short-term, as one specific noncrisis after another is nipped in the bud, and then the next one emerges.

> A different kind of world war, the Cold War was the condition of geo-political tension between Eastern and Western power blocs that began almost immediately after World War II. It was an eerie reminder of the aftermath of World War I, when the issues that caused that earlier conflict continued to fester. Historians say that the Cold War ended with the dissolution of the USSR in 1991, though it appears to continue to this day.

As did Gandhi, Hammarskjöld suffered an ironic assassination—a man of peace killed by violence. Leading a U.N. mission to the Congo to negotiate a cease-fire in the crisis following that country's liberation from Belgium, Hammarskjöld and his fifteen colleagues died in a plane crash in Northern Rhodesia sometime in the overnight hours of September 17–18, 1961. Suspicions surrounded the event from the beginning. New information surfaced in 2017 saying it was "plausible" that the plane had been shot down, but there is still no definitive answer.

I quote President Kennedy's statement expressing his and the country's "deep sense of shock and loss" at Hammarskjöld's death:

> Dag Hammarskjöld's dedication to the cause of peace, his untiring labors to achieve it, his courage under attack, his willingness to accept all responsibility in trying to strengthen the United Nations and make it a more

effective instrument for the aspirations of the hundreds
of millions of people around the globe who desire to live
out their lives—those efforts of his are well known.

Poignantly, this statement by an American leader who would
die by assassination concludes: "I hope that all of us will recognize the heavy burden that his passing places upon us."

The early years of Gandhi and Hammarskjöld could not
have been more different. With Gandhi, there was uncer-
tainty, tumult, mild chaos. Hard to see how this would lead
to a world-changing decision. With Hammarskjöld, there was
a smooth and orderly upward progression, and greater ease associated with his world-changing decision.

Born in 1869 in the state of Porbandar in coastal western
India, Gandhi grew up in a country with a unique and ancient civilization that had for centuries been colonized and
controlled by various European powers. By the mid-1800s, India became known as the "jewel in the British Crown." The
Gandhi family was large, wealthy, and influential, yet modest
as well. Like his forebears, Gandhi's father held a series of local
administrative positions in the colonial government, culmi-
nating at the time of Gandhi's birth in the prime ministership
of Porbandar. Gandhi's mother—the fourth wife of Gandhi's
father—was a devout adherent of the Pranami faith. She was
intensely focused on an intimate relationship with the divine
and spent much time in prayer and fasting.

Young Mohandas was far from a remarkable child—not
really intellectually gifted and, in fact, considered ugly, though
he seemed to possess a certain charm. He admired his worldly
father's power and at the same time was very close to his religious mother. Spoiled, the youngest of two daughters and two
sons, he lived a fairly normal Indian life, which included the
custom of early marriage, in his case at age thirteen (his bride
was also thirteen). Within three years they were parents.

Gandhi's father died in 1885, shortly before Gandhi himself became a father. The combined death/birth experience was emotionally shocking. At the same time, the status of the family plummeted. It was already rocky, because Gandhi's father had been transferred to a less desirable Indian state. London and the study of law beckoned to the young Gandhi, the better to equip him to support his large extended family.

By 1891, Gandhi was back in India, ready to practice law. There he found that, for fear of upsetting him and preventing him from successfully finishing his studies, his family had kept the news of his mother's death from him.

The beginning of Gandhi's legal career was inauspicious; too tongue-tied to cross-examine a witness, he failed miserably in his first court appearance. Through connections, he was soon on his way to a different kind of legal job in South Africa, to help him get his bearings before returning to India and, again, taking up his responsibilities there. You know what happened to him in South Africa, which didn't seem to care that one of her sister countries in the British Empire was considered a "jewel."

Let's turn our attention now to Sweden, where Hammarskjöld was born in 1905, the youngest of four sons, into a favored and "politically elite" family. He grew up in Uppsala, one of the cities of the historic Uppland territory where his father was governor; his father would serve the country as prime minister during World War I. Hammarskjöld was highly influenced by his family's legacy, saying:

> From generations of soldiers and government officials
> on my father's side, I inherited a belief that no life was
> more satisfactory than one of selfless service to your
> country—or humanity. From scholars and clergymen
> on my mother's side, I inherited a belief that, in the
> very radical sense of the Gospels, all men were equals as

children of God, and should be met and treated by us as our masters in God.

Hammarskjöld excelled in all his academic pursuits and in his career of public service. He was a classic "man of parts," defined by Merriam-Webster as a "talented or gifted man, a man of notable endowments or capacity."

He graduated with an honors degree in linguistics, literature, and history from Uppsala University at age twenty. He studied economics and earned his law degree ten years later, also at Uppsala. Moving to Stockholm to take a government position, he continued to study economics and earned his doctorate in 1933 from the University of Stockholm, where he taught for a year. He distinguished himself as he rose through the ranks of Sweden's Ministry of Finance and Ministry of Foreign Affairs. He held the post of chairman of the board of the National Bank of Sweden and was appointed deputy foreign minister in 1951. Domestic and international trade and finance issues, and the diplomacy and negotiations that went along with them, were at the core of his work for Sweden. He never joined a political party.

In 1953, Hammarskjöld was nominated as secretary-general of the United Nations, which had been formed in 1945. He was well known in that young organization, having headed the Swedish delegation to two general assemblies. But his nomination to the top post was almost a universal surprise. After conferring with his father, Hammarskjöld accepted the post, a decision that gave him a unique opportunity to serve and excel globally.

His accomplishments in his seven years as secretary-general were rooted in his belief that quiet (or preventive) diplomacy rather than confrontation was the only moral way to solve conflicts—and more importantly, avoid them. This approach, embedded in the U.N.'s charter, is difficult enough on a small scale, or in homogeneous situations. On a global scale, with size, diversity and history's long memories of grievance, it might seem impossible.

★ ★ ★

Did either of these men of peace win the recognition of the Nobel Peace Prize?

For Hammarskjöld, the answer is short and sweet—yes. The Nobel was awarded to him almost immediately after his death in 1961. This was no knee-jerk reaction in the grief of the moment. Certainly, the secretary-general had his detractors, even deadly enemies (recall the suspicious nature of the fatal place crash). But it seemed necessary that the world immediately honor Hammarskjöld's obvious profound contributions, in the form of the only posthumous action that the Nobel Peace committee had ever taken. Hammarskjöld was cited for the independence he demonstrated in his leadership of the U.N., his peace-keeping work during the Suez crisis of 1956, and his efforts to achieve peace in the Congo—the specific work at the time of his death.

For Gandhi, the answer is also short—no—and not as sweet. Over his long career of activism, he had amassed a multitude of personal and political admirers and enemies; as with Hammarskjöld, recall how the Father of India died. In spite of the efforts of his champions, who nominated him in 1937, 1938, 1939, 1947 and 1948 (days before his assassination), the Nobel distinction was not to be his. There were, however, two Nobel "nods" in Gandhi's direction. The first was the fact that no peace award was made for the year 1948. And the second was that the award to the Dalai Lama in 1989 included this comment by the Nobel committee chairman: "in part a tribute to the memory of Mahatma Gandhi."

The 1896 will of Alfred Nobel—himself a Swedish man of parts—established and funded annual prizes for work in five endeavors: physics, chemistry, physiology/ medicine, literature, and peace. Economics was added in 1968 as a separately-funded honor. Each prize is administered by a separate body (at the time of his death, Hammarskjöld was a member of the Swedish Academy, the arbiter of the literature prize). Prizes do not have to be awarded every year in every category. In 1974, the informal preference of not making awards posthumously was made official policy; prior to that, only Hammarskjöld and one other person had the distinction.

There is no evidence that Gandhi and Hammarskjöld ever met, but can you imagine their conversation if they had? These two complex men shared a core similarity that transcended their different eras and different cultures, their different races and religions. It inspired their leadership, Gandhi using satyagraha and Hammarskjöld using diplomacy.

Hubert Humphrey put it well in a speech he gave called "Gandhi's Living Legacy" at the Dag Hammarskjöld College in Washington, D.C., on November 18, 1969: "The associations are easy to trace. There is a clear philosophic succession from the man who brought the concept of nonviolence into the political arena to the man who sought to institutionalize nonviolence among nations. Both men devoted heart and mind to goals still paramount on the human agenda."

This "philosophic succession" was clearly rooted in the two men's spirituality, which they inherited from their mothers and developed through their unique experiences. Any individual's spirituality, of course, is deeply personal and cannot be grasped by the outside observer. But its results can be; witness the lives and accomplishments of Gandhi and Hammarskjöld. No armchair theorists, they were men of action who put their convictions into practice.

This chapter opened with a quote from Hammarskjöld on his experience of the nature of decisions. It is taken from the book of journal entries and other personal writings published after his death, *Markings*. One can draw a sense of mystical spirituality from his words. So I will end with a statement attributed to Gandhi when a follower asked his advice on decision-making. There is a sense of concrete spirituality in the Mahatma's words:

"Whenever you are in doubt apply the following test. Recall the face of the poorest and weakest man you have seen and ask yourself if the step you contemplate is going to be of any use to him. Will he gain anything by it? Will it restore him control over his own life and destiny?"

Here are the major decision-making lessons for you to think about from Gandhi and Hammarskjöld:

1. Do what is right, regardless of the cost. But recognize that you need to survive and take steps to make sure you do.

2. Identify your enemies and respect them . . . but never let them get the upper hand.

3. Be alert and aware of all of your experiences and influences.

4. Be flexible in assessing situations; some require immediate action, others can wait.

5. Know what your core values are. Project them.

6. Be aware of how your decisions will affect others, either directly or by the example they set.

7. Know when it is time to reflect and assess, and when it is time to get out of your armchair and put your theories to work.

8. Recognize that if you do what is right you will, in the end, prevail.

5

MARGARET THATCHER

> I have already come to the conclusion that I shall
> have to take most of the major decisions myself.
> —MARGARET THATCHER

"HARD-DRIVING AND HARD-HEADED," said *The New York Times*
in its obituary of Lady Margaret Thatcher on April 8, 2013.
Speaking ill of the dead? Not really.

Viewed by some as the reincarnation of the iconic Queen
Elizabeth I and saddled with the label "The Iron Lady," Margaret Thatcher needed those attributes and more as prime minister of Great Britain. When she took office in 1979, her country
had seemingly fallen into permanent decline. When she lost
her last election and her service ended in 1990, she must have
been satisfied that her country had regained its international
stature. Obviously, she presided over many successful decisions.

So, when Margaret Thatcher—a world leader whom I have
long admired—writes in her autobiography that one of her
best decisions was to marry her husband, Denis Thatcher, I
wondered—what about the other decisions that must have been
good ones? Which decisions were in fact world-changing?

Let's look at the first significant decision that tested her met-
tle as prime minister—actually a series of decisions—her adroit
handling of the eleven-week Falklands War against Argentina
in April-May-June of 1982. Had Great Britain not prevailed in
that conflict, it is doubtful that its domestic and international
stature would have recovered. It is likely that Thatcher's three-
year-old prime ministership and political career would have
been over.

Let's set the stage. What kind of woman was Margaret Thatcher, and how did this shape her ability to make the decisions necessary to wage a successful war?

Like Malala Yousafzai, whom I write about in the last chapter of this book, Thatcher was strongly influenced by her father, Alfred Roberts. Not necessarily in her career choice (though she absorbed the example he set in local political service in their town of Grantham, in Lincolnshire), but more for the personal characteristics that he imprinted onto her. In response to a reporter's question as she stepped into No. 10 Downing Street in May 1979, newly elected as prime minister, Thatcher said, "I just owe almost everything to my own father."

Formally uneducated beyond the age of thirteen, Mr. Roberts was a small-town grocer and eventually, a local officeholder and a lay Methodist preacher. He was strict in all aspects of his own life and his expectations of his daughters. He seemed to enjoy little but work. One of Thatcher's biographers noted that "Margaret's upbringing was an unnaturally restricted one, shaped by straitened circumstances and strait-laced parents."

The Roberts family (wife Beatrice, as strict as her husband; mother-in-law Phoebe Stephenson, from whom Beatrice inherited her strictness; daughters Muriel, born in 1921, and Margaret, born in 1925) lived "above the shop." This was a handy location because grocery work demanded morning-to-night hours and six-day weeks. When she was old enough, Margaret worked "behind the counter" (a mahogany barrier, basically, that was kept highly polished, and which she would use gracefully in her autobiography as a metaphor for her life).

Margaret did not have an easy upbringing, rather an austere one, especially as the Depression years turned into the Hitler era and World War II. And as even simple household pleasures were denied—radio programs with music could not be listened to, but news and talk could be. Vacations and "downtime" were unknown. "Work" defined young Margaret's life, and came to be one of her hallmarks as an adult.

The seventh day of the Roberts' family week was devoted to worship. Mr. Roberts was an active lay minister in the Methodist Church, preaching at several services in various locations along his "circuit" every Sunday, always accompanied by family. (Interestingly, music was a feature of these Sunday services.) His lack of formal education notwithstanding, Mr. Roberts had become well-read, liked to write, and enjoyed a reputation as a compelling speaker. His own political career, also marked by daily round-the-clock demands from constituents, began in 1927 when he was an "independent ratepayer." He later became an alderman, serving for ten years, and Grantham's mayor for a year in the 1940s.

Margaret's ambitions for herself lay beyond Grantham and the family business, accessible only by education. She had assistance every step of the way from very necessary scholarships. Her early education, graduation from Oxford in 1947 and a degree in chemistry ("the way of the future," she thought) led to four years of employment as a research chemist with several firms in and around London. And independence. Money for such pleasures as nice outfits and hairdressing was as tight as it was back in Grantham, but her biographies give the sense that Margaret was beginning to enjoy herself. But the tug of politics was always there, in her early years at home, in school, and in university, and as she began her career.

Margaret was introduced to Denis Thatcher in 1949 by mutual friends whom she knew through her political-committee activities. Not a politician himself, not the child of a shopkeeper, and not dependent on scholarships, Denis was a previously married war veteran also educated in chemistry. He was the scion of a family that owned a large paint business called Atlas Preservatives. And he was "comfortably off."

In fact, Thatcher's biographies give a sense that Denis's financial attributes made him a "good catch" for an ambitious young woman with scant material resources herself. Her autobiography focuses on the unfailing support he gave her at every turn of their life together.

The two became engaged in the midst of Margaret's first campaign for office, in 1951, but hid this fact for fear that voters might think that a soon-to-be-married woman was not serious.

Regardless, she lost the election, abandoned chemistry, and promptly married Denis. A very short period of "idleness" followed, and then Margaret began studying law. She "juggled," in today's word, motherhood with her own commitments and Denis's career as eventual CEO of Atlas Preservatives and, after its sale, as a nonexecutive director of numerous companies. Their twin daughter and son were born in 1953 and Margaret was "called to the Bar" in 1954. After five years of law practice and political activity, she decisively won election to Parliament in 1959 and left the legal profession. Twenty years later, she became prime minister, the first woman to hold that position in the Western world.

Barely a week into office, in a speech welcoming German Chancellor Helmut Schmidt, her first head-of-state visitor, Thatcher set forth clearly her governing philosophy: "I intend to be very discriminating in judging what are British interests and I shall be resolute in defending them."

The events in the Falklands fit squarely in this world view.

The 4,700-square mile Falklands, considered a British Overseas Territory, are an archipelago of two large and almost 800 smaller islands in the South Atlantic Ocean. They lie 300 miles off the shore of Argentina and 8,000 miles away from England. They are 850 miles north of the Arctic Circle. They have the climate, geography, flora, and fauna that reflect their setting, and their people possess a very independent spirit. Even today, the home page of the official government website says, "The Falklands Islands is a self-sufficient country. . . . We people of the Falklands Islands have the right to self-determination, enshrined in international law."

But what a history the Falklands have! The Portuguese first sighted the islands in the 1600s. French explorers came upon the uninhabited islands in 1794, then British explorers the next year who named them after a town in Scotland. In 1770, the Spanish arrived to take possession and to begin a long series of skirmishes with the British. At various times, Argentina would claim them and rename them the Malvinas, but control always reverted to the British. At some point, a kind of dormancy descended. When Margaret Thatcher became prime minister, the Islands and their 1,800 citizens could be considered just a tiny remnant of the time when it was said that "the sun never sets on the British Empire."

But nothing is static for very long. Changes in the late 1970s and early 1980s made the islands a newly attractive playing field for both Argentine and British nationalism, and important enough to merit a war over who would possess them.

On the Argentine side, a new dictatorship sought economic and international legitimacy. On the British side, ceding control of even an iota of the Empire was anathema to its national identity and certainly counter to Thatcher's governing philosophy of resolute defense.

The timeline of the Falklands War presents a fairly clear picture of provocation by Argentina; reaction by the Great Britain; "assistance" of one kind or another by the United States, France, and the United Nations; the brooding presence in the background of the Soviet Union, and a citizenry caught in the middle.

Here is a timeline of the three-month war:

March 19, 1992—First Argentine incursion on the islands, in the form of an unauthorized landing by scrap-metal ships

April 2—Invasion by Argentine military forces

April 3—Argentina continues to push forward, the UN is involved

April 5—First British forces "set sail"

April 15—The UK begins to re-take the island

May 1, 2, 4—Bombing and missile strikes by British forces

May 14, 15—Additional successful British raids on Argentine forces

May 20—UN peace talks fail

May 21, 23, 25—Three British vessels are sunk

June 1–14—Aggressive fighting on both sides

June 14—Argentina surrenders

History is neater in hindsight. Once we know the outcome of, say, a war, it is easier to identify and analyze its causes, the characters of the people waging it, the strategic decisions and so on. But history as it unfolds is a different matter.

As it was with the Falklands War. I can see the crescendo of events in a more complete way than Thatcher ever could, because I know the outcome and she did not. What she did know was that she had to bring every ounce of her character, her intelligence, and her vision for Great Britain to bear upon the threat that faced the country's sovereignty.

Margaret Thatcher was the first woman to hold the office of prime minister in Great Britain. Is Thatcher's gender relevant to our consideration of her decisions in the Falklands War?

I feel almost foolish posing the question *Did she have what it takes?* But it continues to be asked, of every woman seeking to lead and achieve in government, corporations, universities, the media, law firms, medicine, the military, science, and so on— every endeavor outside of the home.

And Thatcher faced questions of gender from the very beginning of her political and legal careers. She herself wrote that "there was a great deal of suspicion of women candidates. . . this was quite definitely a man's world into which not just angels feared to tread." Remember her unannounced engagement to Denis during her first campaign? During that era any female candidate would have had a difficult time begin elected, but an unmarried, unattached woman was possibly more acceptable. Also tax law (Thatcher's specialty) was deemed more "suitable" for a married woman with children than anything involving litigation.

On the personal side, Thatcher's answer to any questions about her competency was the "work-work-work," results-oriented approach that marked her childhood and her whole life. And on the larger, societal side, that was her answer too— she just didn't pay much attention whether or not she was viewed as a feminist.

Regarding leadership in the British success in the Falklands, I'll point out that Margaret Thatcher had no choice but to lead. Her gender did not matter. I'll also point out a cliché: The proof is in the pudding—results speak for themselves. (Clichés may be truisms but they are born from truths; before they were hackneyed, they were original.)

Another factor in the Falklands war was the gap between people who had actual wartime experience and those who had none. Margaret Thatcher had no military experience. Her World War II–veteran husband did, but most of her other advisors did not. Almost a generation had passed since the end of World War II, the British involvement in the Korean War, and the humiliating resolution of the Suez Crisis. Relevant military experience was in short supply.

What's important here is that Thatcher possessed the prerequisites of an effective decision-maker. She had a secure and well-formed character. She had "life experience." She had a well-articulated philosophy. She had numerous advisors and knew how to sift through their advice. She had a vision of what could and should be accomplished short- and long-term. These are all strong attributes.

Another strong attribute was that she seemed to know that she did not know everything she needed to know. From Charles Moore's official biography:

> [Thatcher] was obviously at a disadvantage in knowing nothing about war . . . But there was a less obvious sense in which her lack of knowledge helped. It gave her the humility which she was often, in other matters, accused of lacking, and encourages her to listen to colleagues . . . It also kept her mind clear for the political task and made her uncomplicatedly anxious to do everything possible for the [military forces].

But there was, for a female nonveteran commander-in-chief, a more problematical side to Thatcher's inexperience. This Moore quote from an apparent nonfan of Thatcher's summed up what may have been a prevailing attitude:

> She wouldn't have done it if she had been a man and if she'd been in the armed forces during the war. Then she'd have been aware how dreadfully wrong everything was likely to go.

Nothing much did go "dreadfully wrong" in the Falklands War after all. But this was a very fraught time politically for Thatcher, one when she felt "isolation" and "loneliness" and was "more or less on her own," especially as she tended to all the other issues demanding her leadership.

There are many similarities between Harry Truman and

Margaret Thatcher. Earlier, I spoke of the loneliness inherent in the U.S. president's position as he faced the decision to use the nuclear bomb. Surrounded by advisors, allies, enemies, battle plans, projections of casualties and myriad other data points, Truman alone had the final responsibility. Thatcher faced the same conditions. And she had her version of "the buck stops here." She assumed "most of the major decisions myself," not as a whining complaint but as a fact of life whose burden she seemed to welcome.

A sense of breathlessness comes through to me from both contemporary news accounts of the Falklands War and the more considered history books, biographies, and memoirs available today. There was little time for reflection. The war was conducted at almost breakneck speed. Many decisions seem to have been be made on the fly, with little chance to evaluate the consequences before another set of decisions careened into the mix. And it was all complicated by the fact that the war was being waged in rugged weather (early winter in the Southern Hemisphere near the Antarctic) practically on the doorstep of the enemy—8,000 miles from where Thatcher presided. Just as Truman sat in Washington, some 7,000 miles from Japan.

One might say that the stakes for Thatcher were not as high as for Truman, that there was no proportionality between the decisions they faced. But the foundational question was the same—What was the right thing to do?

It would be unnatural to assume that Thatcher was properly decisive every minute of every day. Biographer Moore cited the "byways of minutiae" that she "hurried off down" during this time. That behavior may have been characteristic at other times, too, as he noted that it "was her wont when she was under stress."

It was two years after the Argentine surrender that Thatcher was able to travel to the Falklands for the first time. Surely the victory had been tinged with sadness for Thatcher. Inexperienced in warfare though she was, she was fully aware of the human cost in casualties. One can see that weight in her posture as she was photographed, alone save for a military aide at her side, bending to lay a wreath at the cemetery at San Carlos Bay. On the British side, there were 255 dead and 777 wounded, all military. On the Argentine side, 648 military and one civilian (who was serving as a sailor) dead and 1,188 wounded. And three Falkland women civilians died in "friendly fire."

Today, the Falklands remain an independent country that is part of the United Kingdom. Periodically, tensions arise with Argentina that are quelled by the fact that the Islanders themselves (now a population of about 3,400) prefer the status quo, as they did in 1981.

After the Falklands War, Thatcher's popularity initially soared, and the UK's reputation began to be restored. As one would expect, Thatcher was a vigorous leader in her remaining eight years as prime minister. I get the strong sense that she was almost crushed when she was turned out of office in 1990; there was so much more she wanted to do on the British and the world stages. But voters decide.

Let me conclude with a look at another possible similarity between Harry Truman and Margaret Thatcher.

In the beginning of this chapter, I raised the subject of Margaret's citation of marrying Denis Thatcher as "one of my best decisions." Her autobiography speaks so warmly of a husband who seemed to be the very definition of that arcane term "helpmeet" but also her equal in all ways. In an interview on the occasion of their thirty-fifth wedding anniversary, in 1986, Margaret called Denis "a golden thread" running through her life. One thinks of Harry and Bess. Though I am as reluctant to analyze the Thatchers' marriage as I was the Trumans', it is clear to me that the existence of intimate partnerships plays a key role in successful decision-making.

★ ★ ★

Here's what I suggest we can take away about decision-making, based on Margaret Thatcher and the Falklands War:

1. Have the courage of your conviction. Many elements may stand in your way. If what you want to do is right, just go for it and be creative in terms of the way you achieve your success.

2. Seek advice from knowledgeable sources—and listen to it. You don't have to follow it, but you need to have it. If others have experience that you lack, explore what they have already learned in similar circumstances. And remember that people you reach out to, can become you biggest fans and help carry out the decisions you make.

3. Pause, if you can. This may give you time to think "outside the box." I said earlier that I had the impression of Margaret Thatcher making decisions at almost headlong speed. Undoubtedly the situation called for that, but thankfully few of us are making decisions in wartime.

4. Always think about the implications of your decisions. Do you play chess, backgammon, cards, or even checkers? All these games rely on thinking beyond the immediate or most obvious move. The safety and well-being of individual people must always be considered. But your decisions may also need to take into account the environment, the markets, your industry and so much more. The people whose stories are in this book, for example, made decisions that helped change the world.

5. Do not let prejudice stop you. Many people may hold (and hide) preconceived negative ideas about your race, your gender, your sexual identity, your age, your appearance, your national origin, your faith, your economic status, your level of education and so many other personal characteristics. Even your lack of first-hand wartime experience, as Margaret Thatcher found. They may use these ideas to stand in your way as you make and carry out your decisions.

6. Own your own decisions. Be responsible for them and for their implications. Do not be reactionary—that is, making decisions to spite others or because of outside pressure—but do be respectful of their effect on others.

7. Try as hard as you can to find and form a higher purpose with your decision. When she became Prime Minister, Thatcher declared herself "resolute in defending British interests." While some might have seen the Argentine 1982 incursion onto the Falklands as a dispute or a provocation, Thatcher believed that nothing less than the existence of the British Empire was at stake. I'm not advising you to be grandiose, but don't be afraid of aiming high. Few people really do, and your decisions will stand out.

8. Involve your spouse, partner or significant other as appropriate, or necessary, in your decision-making process. Will what you do affect them, need their involvement? Do they have knowledge and experience that can help you? Do you need moral support, a sympathetic shoulder to lean on, or something more concrete?

6

JOAN OF ARC

> My voices were from God, and everything I did
> was according to God's will.
> —JOAN OF ARC

IMAGINE A TEENAGE GIRL who, because she decided to obey the
orders of divine voices that she alone could hear, changed
the course of French and English history. If we did not have
the historical record from the early fifteenth century that tells
us that this girl, Joan of Arc, was an actual person who really
did live, her story would seem to be a myth. But live, she did.

In addition to being an official French heroine, Joan is a Roman Catholic saint, so I'll turn to Church history for some basic
information. Like many Catholic children growing up in a certain era, I was very fond of a small devotional book called *The
Lives of the Saints*. Because some books cannot be discarded, I
still have my copy in my "archives." The entry on Joan of Arc
may be oversimplified, but it sets the stage. It reads as follows:

> On January 6, 1412, Joan of Arc was born to pious
> parents of the French peasant class, at the obscure village
> of Domremy, near the province of Lorraine. At a very
> early age she heard voices; those of St. Michael, St.
> Catherine, and St. Margaret. At first the messages were
> personal and general. Then at last came the crowning
> order. In May 1428, the voices told Joan to go to the King
> of France and help him reconquer his kingdom. After
> overcoming opposition from churchmen and courtiers,
> she was given a small army with which she raised the siege

of Orleans on May 8, 1429. While defending Compiegne she was taken prisoner and sold to the English. She was judged at Rouen by a tribunal presided over by the infamous Cauchon, Bishop of Beauvais. Although she astounded her judges by the readiness of her answers, she was condemned to death as a heretic, and burned at the stake, May 24 [*sic*; actually May 30], 1431.

Why did the French king need to "reconquer his kingdom"? (In fact, Charles VII had not yet been able to claim his crown; he was still considered only a "dauphin," the eldest son of a king, even though his father had died in 1422.) The reason is embedded in the causes of the Hundred Years' War. This war was a series of battles, disputes, intrigues, sieges, occupations, and various other conflicts, fought almost entirely on French soil, between England and France from 1337 to 1453 (or even longer, depending on the historian). Questions of royal succession (five generations of kings! illegitimate children!) and France's sovereignty (England laid claim to France, then the largest and strongest European country), were the root causes.

Michael the Archangel (St. Michael) is revered in Judaism, Christianity, and Islam. He is invoked for assistance with spiritual battles of all kinds. He is often depicted dressed as a mighty winged soldier spearing to death the horrible serpent that cowers at his feet. A traditional prayer reads, in part, "Michael the Archangel, defend us in battle, be our protection. . . ." Saints Margaret and Catherine were revered as martyrs who had been convicted and executed because they would not recant their Christian faith.

When Joan was sent by the yet-uncrowned Charles VII to Orleans in 1429 at age seventeen, the king was desperate. He must have figured that nothing worse could happen to him or his country. Complete chaos ruled, as it had for generations. The entire French war effort was teetering on the brink of total defeat. Where could he turn? Here was a girl who said that God had been speaking to her for four years, through the voices of at least three saints. What did Charles VII have to lose?

Joan's participation in the collapse of the five-month-long siege and the freeing of Orleans was both morally inspirational to the French and militarily significant. It turned the tide of war, as more French victories followed. It took at least another twenty-plus years, but the French shook off the English. The long national nightmare, to paraphrase an American president in another context, was over.

> The end of the Hundred Years' War was not France's last experience with occupation by enemy forces. The two world wars of the twentieth century come immediately to mind.
>
> Interestingly, the United States enlisted Joan of Arc—her iconic image and aura—in our World War I fundraising effort. The initial supply of war bonds had been received so enthusiastically that it had sold out. While a new issue was being prepared, the Treasury Department devised a place-saving product that was marketed directly at women. On a now famous poster, a beautiful, vibrant and armor-clad Joan appears with these words: "Joan of Arc Saved France. Women of America. Save Your Country. Buy War Savings Stamps."

What did Joan earn from her effort? As my childhood devotional book says, she ended up in the hands of the enemy. She was tried and found guilty as a heretic because she would not recant that her voices had come from the angels and the saints and therefore from God. She was executed by being burned at the stake, a common punishment for heretics in the Middle Ages. Let's remember, she was nineteen.

Almost immediately, Joan became a heroine of the French nation and a cult developed around her. At the time of the Hundred Years' War's end, her case was re-examined. Posthumously she was absolved of the charges that had led to her execution. Canonization by the Catholic Church took place in 1920.

The importance of Joan cannot be understood without taking a look at the place of Christianity in France—and in all of Europe—at Joan's time. Christianity and Catholicism were synonymous. Quite simply, the Catholic Church in the form of the Holy Roman Empire ruled alongside the kings and queens; it was intertwined with all official life. Personal life, too. "Everybody" was Catholic, including the combatants of the Hundred Years' War. Remember, that war was not a conflict over religion; its purpose was the acquisition of land and therefore power. But Joan being ordered by divine sources to assist Charles VII certainly could be viewed as God taking sides in a family dispute.

In 1517, less than a century after Joan's death, the Christian Catholic façade in Europe began to crack. That year, in Germany, Martin Luther published his Ninety-Five Theses, inspiring the struggles of the Protestant Reformation that lasted until the end of the Thirty Years' War in 1648. Yes, another long war, one that began over religious issues but then grew to involve every other issue you could imagine and every country in Europe. After horrible carnage (deaths estimated at eight million), the war ended with the Treaty of Westphalia redrawing most every national boundary and establishing individual nations' sovereignty. The days of the Holy Roman Empire were over. In France, Catholicism was re-affirmed as that country's national religion, but not so in other countries. England, for example, had broken with Rome back in 1534, when King Henry VIII famously defied the Pope and founded the Church of England, which is to this day considered the "established" church in that country. In Germany and Switzerland, the combined efforts of Luther, John Calvin, Huldrych Zwingli and many others developed into the diverse so-called "Protestant" branches of Christianity.

In Catholic parlance, because "the faith" came to France very early (in the second century), France is called "the eldest daughter of the Church." But France's official Catholicism ended after the French Revolution in 1788–89, a position buttressed by the 1905 law on the Separation of the Churches and State.

Today, Joan of Arc's country is considered secular or multiconfessional, and prides itself on its religious tolerance. Approximately 65 percent of France's 67 million citizens identify as Christian (80 percent of that figure represents Catholics, only 5 percent of whom "worship regularly"). Of the remaining 35 percent or so of the population, the largest single group is Islam, 7 percent and growing. Smaller percentages are represented by Judaism, Buddhism, Russian Orthodoxy, and Sikhism.

I daresay that few people care that Joan of Arc is one of France's ten patron saints (the Catholic Church endows all countries with patron saints). But type "heroes of France" into your search engine, and you will see that Joan has a secure place among luminaries such as Victor Hugo, the Marquis de Lafayette, Charles de Gaulle, Claude Monet, Napoleon, Louis Pasteur, Gustav Eiffel, and other military, cultural, scientific, political, and business leaders.

Regardless of the historical facts of Joan's life and military career, many thoughtful people view the Maid of Orleans largely as a myth or a fantasy, or at least a psychologically troubled person. They are suspicious of her motives. They doubt the existence of Joan's voices. Or they have their own interpretations about the origin of the voices. The list includes George

Bernard Shaw, whose most famous drama is the iconic Saint Joan. Historian Donald Spoto quoted from the play to introduce his own book *Joan*:

> JOAN: I heard voices tell me what to do. They come from
>   God.
> ROBERT: They come from your imagination.
> JOAN: Of course. That is how messages of God come
>   to us.

(Let's keep in mind that plays are works of imagination!)

Spoto also quoted Joan herself days before her execution: "My voices were from God, and everything I did was according to God's will."

Vita Sackville-West, whose biography *Saint Joan of Arc* is quite focused on Joan's psychology, said that "her single-mindedness" may have been her most important quality. Joan also had

> the power to accomplish what she had undertaken.
> Her courage and conviction were superhuman. They
> were of the quality which admits no doubt and
> recognized no obstacle. Her own absolute faith was the
> secret of her strength.

I am not going to weigh into a discussion of Joan's spirituality, psychology, or motivation. What I will weigh into, is what Joan of Arc's story means for decision-making for you and for me.

We all hear inner voices. I am not speaking of the "auditory hallucinations" that are a recognized diagnostic factor in schizophrenia. I am speaking of the "chatter" that goes on in our minds about . . . whether or not to eat another donut for breakfast, to turn left at the next intersection, to take an umbrella when we leave the house on a rainy day—all sorts of trivial or useful things. And there is the more vital chatter that goes on and on; for example, planning what we are going to say at an important meeting or revising with second thoughts a meeting that was disappointing. And then there is the most vital chatter of all—what we say to ourselves and what we hear in our inner selves, when we are trying to make a decision.

This last kind of chatter is immensely important. We owe it to ourselves to pay attention to it and to hone it, so it is of the highest quality. It needs to be reliable, grounded in both reality and imagination. This is often called the process of "discernment," separating as it were the wheat from the chaff.

I think that the Maid of Orleans, as young and uneducated and unformed as she was, went through her own discernment process during the four years that her voices spoke to her before she went off to find Charles VII. Any of us can become discerning persons:

1. Always seek a higher and a positive purpose.

2. Pay attention to your innermost thoughts, feelings, impulses, likes/dislikes and so on. Don't necessarily act on them, but view them as guideposts toward what's important.

3. Expose yourself to as much knowledge as possible, and diverse, informed opinion from others. Read broadly, listen to many sources and observe all that is around you. Learn!

4. Ask for help. Joan's uncle was instrumental in helping her travel to Charles VII.

5. When facing a decision, play out all sides. Imagine (in detail and with sincerity) going in one direction with your decision and see how that feels. Then the other. And a third or fourth if they exist. You will discover that one probably feels more "right" than the others.

6. If you are a "person of faith," pray for the full development of your conscience, the arbiter of what is right and wrong.

7. Sackville-West wrote of Joan's "single-mindedness" and "courage and conviction." Once you have set your course and are executing your decisions, make these qualities work for you, too.

8. Do not be afraid to dream.

PART TWO
Commerce and Invention

7

JOHANN GUTENBERG

> What the world is today, good and bad, it owes to
> Gutenberg. Everything can be traced to this source.
> —MARK TWAIN

NO ONE QUESTIONS THE FACT that, with his dual inventions of
movable type and the printing press in the middle of the fifteenth century, Johann Gutenberg changed the world.

Intriguingly, he likely had no clue! His life's goal was to
make money and all of his decisions were geared that way. No
high-minded and enlightened visions guided him. He had no
thoughts of "making everyone a reader," to paraphrase Marshall McLuhan's statement about him five centuries later. And
the object that symbolizes his achievement—the Gutenberg
Bible—was nearly credited to someone else.

Gutenberg's story fascinates me because it breaks the mold
of what one would expect. I think that this inventor from the
Middle Ages offers strong lessons in modern decision-making.

John Man, author of *Gutenberg: How One Man Remade the
World with His Words,* and several other books on Gutenberg
and the revolution of printing, speaks of his own "preconcep-
tions" about the inventor:

> If printing was one of the foundations of the modern
> world, then—I had supposed—Gutenberg had to be a
> selfless genius, in the vanguard of modernity, dedicated
> to improving the world, eager to bring to it the benefits
> of new knowledge. Not a bit. The truth, it seems to me,
> is the precise opposite of my preconceptions. Gutenberg's

aim, I believe, was that of a businessman striving to
be the first to cash in on the Continent-wide market
offered by the Catholic Church.

Little is known about Gutenberg's life. He was born and baptized in Mainz, Germany, sometime between 1394 and 1404,
but history has settled on 1400. He lived mostly in Mainz and
Strasbourg, Germany, but spent some time in France. He died
in Mainz in 1468, probably on February 3.

His father Friele was a "Companion of the Mint" (a high-
level employee in perhaps the key governmental institution in
Mainz, literally where the money was made). This was an occupation of status and influence that he had inherited from
his own father, and he was considered a patrician. However,
Friele "married down," to use an ugly phrase. His wife Else's
family, which had enjoyed some gentility and means in the
past, had lost its position as the result of some forebear making
the wrong decision about a civil war. The family no longer
qualified as "rich" or particularly well-placed; her father had
become a shopkeeper. Given the realities, then and now, of
social stratification, this disparity between paternal and mater-
nal status "threw shade" (as we might say now) on Johann, his
younger sister, and his older brother, none of whom would be
able to inherit the "Companion of the Mint" sinecure (though
Johann did work at the mint for a period of time).

Young Johann was intelligent and probably had a good
education, though not one geared to a specific profession or
calling. Mainz abounded in schools for children and universities, most run by orders of Catholic priests and monks, so he
knew how to read and would have been steeped in doctrine
and Latin. Whether he emerged from the experience a pious
Christian I do not know, but he remains inextricably linked to
the Church.

As he entered young adulthood, Gutenberg wanted to lead
a comfortable life and was ambitious to make money. He
could not permanently follow in his father's footsteps at the

mint, and the financial inheritance he should have received after Friele's death was not fully available to him, fifteenth century law being what it was. Luckily, he had lots of ideas to address his situation, and we will see how some of these played out.

> Gutenberg was born Johann (or Johannes) Gens-fleisch. As was common then, he adopted the name of his father's house as his own. (It was also common to name houses.) There is some speculation that he did not like the fact that Gensfleisch translated to "goose meat" or "goose flesh."

I said that we know little about Gutenberg. What *is* known can be pieced together, with a little imagination, from two main sources:

First, knowledge of conditions in Germany, and in all of Europe, in the first half of the fifteenth century. Plagues, wars, chaos of all kinds abounded; several times in Gutenberg's youth, his family had to withdraw from the city to safety. Mainz, his birthplace, constantly teetered on financial disaster. Craft and merchant guilds ruled the business world, and were in conflict with patricians such as Gutenberg's father. Political power resided with the Holy Roman Empire and the Catholic Church (both Roman and Orthodox), with leaders from all sides alternately cooperating with and battling each other. Germany was still more of a collection of small cities and town rather than a nation, but it did have a king trying to instill unity. A hundred or so years into the Renaissance, knowledge of all kinds was beginning to flow, but was still largely concentrated among the privileged few. (Note that this was the world that Joan of Arc was born into, in France in 1412.)

Second, there were plentiful records, many of them financial documents and lawsuits, resulting from Gutenberg's constant attempts to make money. He was often being sued, avoiding bankruptcy, making and breaking partnerships, moving from one city to another and so on. We can track where he was (mostly; he often "disappeared" after a bankruptcy) and what he was doing (mostly; he liked to work in secret).

In case you are wondering if Gutenberg had a wife and a family, the answer is unknown. The only clue is a breach-of-promise suit brought by Ellewibel, the mother of a young lady named Ennelin. Whether there really had been a promise, whether Ellewibel was more interested in her daughter marrying Gutenberg than was the daughter herself, whether Gutenberg knew that a marriage was even expected, whether Ellewibel was as ambitious for money as was Gutenberg, the outcome of the marriage suit—all this is lost information. We do know that Gutenberg insulted the witness that Ellewibel brought forward; the witness successfully sued Gutenberg for defamation.

Some ideas are like Newton's falling apple or the birth of Athena from Zeus's forehead—they arrive, fully formed and obvious. Most ideas, like Gutenberg's, take the Beatles' "long and winding road." Experiences and influences; dreams, experiments, and failures; dogged hard work and serendipity—all these factors and more provide the fertile ground that can turn ideas into reality. In Gutenberg's case, a constellation of factors was unique to his life and milieu. The decisions he made about those factors assured that his ideas would turn into world-changing inventions.

Had Gutenberg invented *either* movable type *or* the printing press, he would be celebrated. But his combination of the two into one—that was his genius. Gutenberg's work enabled the production of large amounts of standardized printed material in a relatively short time, material that could be distributed easily. This meant that knowledge could be shared, not closely held. Gutenberg perfected his techniques in 1450 and began printing books two years later. By the turn of the century, more than ten million individual books existed in Europe.

So, let's take a look at the canny set of decisions Gutenberg made to advance his ideas into reality, a reality that changed the world.

It's important to understand that Gutenberg did not invent printing. Humans had long known how to carve images onto blocks, usually wooden, apply ink to the blocks and impress the inked block by hand onto a piece of paper, leaving the image behind. A pretty cumbersome process. Suitable as an art form, certainly, but not conducive to easily and quickly conveying information. The Chinese and the Koreans had long been appreciated for their elegant work in this type of printing.

It's also important to understand that in Gutenberg's time there was little interest in conveying information, quickly or otherwise. Or in standardizing information. The main repository of knowledge was the Roman Catholic Church, which closely guarded her perquisites. While each clerical community had its own holy documents, these were not commonly shared among communities and certainly not with the general population. What needed to be read was prepared by hand, one at a time, painstakingly, by scribes and illuminators who ultimately created the uncommonly beautiful art objects known as "illuminated manuscripts." Under these conditions, however, even a book such as the Bible would differ slightly from community to community.

Gutenberg, always on the lookout for "the main chance," was aware of efforts, led by the German Cardinal Nicholas Cusa in 1448, to make the Bible itself more available to the faithful. This was part of a larger effort to unify the silos of knowledge contained in individual Catholic communities, not only in Germany but across Europe. Gutenberg decided, essentially, to back Cardinal Cusa in his quest. He agreed that "religious truth is imprisoned in a small number of manuscript books which confine instead of spread the public treasure." One of the first orders of business: to move beyond the limitations of hand-written Bibles, tracts, hymnals and other devotional material, including the soon-to-be infamous "indulgences."

Gutenberg decided that he had the answer.

By the time Cardinal Cusa came along, Gutenberg had been experimenting with type and printing for close to thirty years. Think of this as an extended period of product development to address a market that Gutenberg viewed as ready-made, though frustrating.

Gutenberg already had experience with the potential financial opportunity represented by the Church. Specifically, the many hordes of faithful pilgrims who traveled to the Holy Land and other sites to view relics. It was believed that wearing a shiny piece of metal when near a relic would cause the spiritual power of the relic to be reflected onto the wearer. In 1437, Gutenberg jumped wholesale into the production of these little "pilgrim mirrors" for the annual religious festival held in Strasbourg, where he was then living. (Recall his and his father's work at the Mainz mint. Gutenberg was familiar with working with metal, casting it, inscribing it, making it useful.)

Using what he knew, seeing a ready market and imagining only expansion, Gutenberg was initially a successful supplier of these spiritual aids. But an outbreak of the oft-recurring plague in 1439 cancelled the Strasbourg festival. All of a sudden, Gutenberg had no customers. (He did have one of his many bankruptcies.) He was, as usual, undeterred in his search for monetary success and, just about a decade later, was quite ready to apply his experiments with type and printing presses to Cardinal Cusa's priorities.

The development of movable type and its mechanical application was that "long and winding road" I referred to earlier. Using individual letters, rather than pictograms or blocks of text, assured flexibility, as the letters could be arranged and rearranged at will. And if they were permanently cast into long-lasting metal, not carved into wood that, no matter how hard, is still a soft, easily dulled material, the letters could be re-used again and again. The traditional Chinese and Korean ink and paper was not suitable for contact with metal, so new kinds of ink and paper had to be formulated. And the traditional method of hand-stamping was not suitable either. But could a machine do the work? What about adapting the presses equipped with giant screws and plates that squeezed olives into oil and grapes into juice and eventually wine?

Eventually, Gutenberg devised a system of slotting individual letters and punctuation symbols made of lead into orderly rows on frames laid flat in a printing press, with ink applied and a sheet of paper laid over all. When the sheet was removed, there was a page of the Bible, there was the text of a psalm, there was an indulgence form—or anything else you wanted. Then another sheet could be laid down on the same plate and another copy printed; on and on. Meanwhile, on another press, the same process with different lines of type could be printing a different page.

It was still a painstaking, laborious, time-consuming process to print a single page. Physically exhausting, too—think of lifting frames filled with little pieces of lead, think of applying your body weight to turning the giant screws of the presses (motors had not yet been invented). But compared to the handwritten process, Gutenberg's method seemed almost easy and lightning-fast. Moreover, any number of standard copies could be made. The door to the future was open.

During the seemingly endless years of Gutenberg's trial-and-error product development, he did not always have the funds he needed to buy his supplies or secure work space. Nor was it possible to work alone; the tasks were too onerous. He needed loans and he needed people.

So, he made a key decision that, while allowing him to make

progress, also made him vulnerable to lawsuits and suspicion—
he decided to work in secret. Many who lent him money never
saw what he was doing. Many who actually worked with him
never saw the full picture. *Why does the ink need to be just so?
Never mind, just mix it the way I tell you. Why is this kind of paper
suitable and this not? Never mind, just make it according to my for-
mula.* Well, lenders and partners and employees won't generally
stand for this treatment for very long, and Gutenberg was the
target of many legal disputes.

Saddest of all the disputes was the one in 1455 that took away
the print workshop, the business in Mainz, where "the" Bible
had been born. Gutenberg had had to borrow money to keep
the shop afloat. The lender—Johann Fust, a long-time partner
whom Gutenberg thought was trustworthy or at least patient—
basically called the loan, probably knowing that it could not be
repaid. Gutenberg's work product was swept up and away as
part of the property settlement associated with the loan. Fust
continued to print Bibles, but they were never of the caliber
of Gutenberg's, whose name was not associated with his own
work until well after his death. It was in 1504 that credit began
to accrue to him, thanks to a professor at Mainz University.

Those of us who love books and reading and communications can easily become enmeshed in the minutia of Gutenberg's compelling inventions, the myriad details that had to
come together in a result that changed the world. So, I'll stop
here; after all this is a book about decision-making, not inventions.

But I can't resist looking at the crowning achievement of
all his decisions—the work of art we now call the Gutenberg
Bible. (Not the Fust Bible or the Mainz Bible.)

Gutenberg grasped that producing "the" Bible, which he
did between 1450 and 1455, would aid the Roman Catholic
Church in her quest for unity and centralized power. That victory was temporary, as the Protestant Reformation would tear

that unity apart beginning in 1517. John Man, whom I quoted earlier, wrote:

It is one of history's greatest ironies that [Gutenberg] achieved exactly the reverse of his intentions. Having succeeded at last, with an astounding display of brilliance and perseverance, he almost lost everything to his partners and colleagues, only by the skin of his teeth avoiding poverty and obscurity. And having produced one of the greatest of Christian publications, he ushered in a revolution—the Reformation—that blew Christian unity apart forever.

One of the reasons that Martin Luther's famous Ninety-Five Theses—an early skirmish in the war that became the Protestant Reformation—became known so quickly is because they were printed, not hand-written. As related in the chapter on Martin Luther in this book, Luther embedded them in what he initially intended to be a private letter to his bishop in 1517. But the printer of the document, apparently sensing its import, distributed the theses publicly.

Gutenberg was not just a technician who invented things that worked well. He was a true creative. He had an eye for beauty and design that was surprising; there was nothing in his background that would account for that trait. He seemed to know, instinctively, just how a carved letter should look, just how long a line of type should be, just how many lines should be on a page—even whether a period or a hyphen that fell at the end of a line should appear within the justified margin or slightly outside of it. All of his aesthetic decisions resulted in printed pages that were as unique as his handwriting; even without his name affixed, ultimately everyone realized that they had his "signature."

And Gutenberg's aesthetic decisions came together in the numerous individual Bibles that he personally designed and printed. History says that Gutenberg produced approximately 180 Bibles (the exact number is not known); twenty-one complete copies still exist, five of them in the United States, along with twenty-eight partial copies and many fragments. There is no one book designated as the "Gutenberg Bible"; we refer to all of them collectively, as if they were all a single volume. Remember, Gutenberg's inventive decision-making changed the world because it enabled, essentially, mass communication.

Did Gutenberg ever achieve the financial success he craved and toward which his decisions were geared? Sort of. After he lost his Bible-based printing business to Fust, he did persevere for close to ten years with another small shop, printing items of little significance. He seemed to have lost heart. But in 1465, the archbishop of Mainz recognized Gutenberg as a "Gentleman of the Court," which entitled him to a "pension" of clothing, wine, and food. Gutenberg lived the final three years of his life comfortably enough.

What can the story of Johann Gutenberg, a money-motivated inventor from six centuries ago, teach us about decision-making in this day and age?

Some lessons are clear, and we have seen them at work with other people profiled in this book:

1. Be clear about your goals! Write them down. Test them with those you trust.

2. Know who or what is the likely target for your ideas. If you are running a business, know your market inside out and tailor your products and activities accordingly. Gutenberg knew that his printed Bibles had to meet or exceed the standards of beauty that an illuminated manuscript version offered.

3. Allow room for influences of all kinds. Your parents' occupations, your childhood pastimes, events in your community, the subjects you loved or hated in school—all these and more can color the decisions you make.

4. Have a fall-back plan. Several. If your initial efforts are not working well or are actually failing, and you have the same goal, find a new way. Instead of pilgrim mirrors, make Bibles. Or find an entirely new goal.

5. Be prepared for conflict and misunderstandings. Gutenberg believed that secrecy was necessary in his R&D work, whether from paranoia or with good cause. This resulted in many problems for him, but didn't make him change his ways. If you need people to help you execute your decisions, treat those people well.

6. Persevere and maintain high standards. Important things are worth doing well. Take the time you need to develop the components of your ideas to their highest form. For Gutenberg, this meant never stinting in the search for the right ink, the best paper, the most pleasing type designs.

Now let me offer some cautionary words about Johann Gutenberg and what I have cited so often as his major goal— to make money. In my life and career, I have found that goal not to be sufficient. Or fully satisfying. Of course, no one sets out to be a financial failure. Like most people, I have sought to make decisions aimed at financial rewards: my education and my choice of a profession, for example. Thanks to good decisions (and in spite of some bad decisions), I have enjoyed running a successful business—for my family's sake, for my colleagues' sakes, for my clients' sakes. And I'll admit, for my own sake, too—my pride, my ego, my sense of the way things should be.

But I believe that making money is an interim goal. The true goal should be much larger and at the same time, much simpler. It is this: your purpose in life. This goal lives in the realm of what is ultimately the most gratifying to you. It takes an intense personal endeavor for you to search for it, recognize it, and then make the decisions so that you can begin to attain it.

I'll be so bold as to say that Gutenberg never achieved his goal. He didn't realize that the purpose in life was not to make money. Any money he made or would have made is long gone now anyway. Even his Bible—"among the most astonishing objects ever created," to cite John Man's words again, "a jewel of art and technology, one that emerged fully formed, of a perfection beyond anything required for its purpose"—was an interim goal. He may never have known it, but Gutenberg's purpose in life was freedom of knowledge, giving humankind the tools necessary for true communication.

8

A. P. GIANNINI

It's no use, however, to decide what's going to
happen unless you have your convictions.
—A. P. GIANNINI

DO YOU HAVE A CHECKING ACCOUNT? A savings account? How
about a car loan or a mortgage? And are you a "regular" person? Then you have been affected by two groundbreaking decisions made a hundred-plus years ago by entrepreneur and
banker A. P. Giannini that are the basis of the system we now
know as "consumer banking."

When Giannini arrived on the scene, banks such as Wells
Fargo, the American National Bank, and the First National
Bank of San Francisco dealt predominantly with wealthy or established people or entities. Most "regular" people who didn't
already have money, or possessions to serve as collateral to get
money, were simply not in the picture. Many of these people
were Italian immigrants, like Giannini's parents, who came to
California from Italy in the mid-1800s. How do you get a start
if you have little or nothing to start with?

Giannini absorbed his family's experiences. He saw the prejudice that immigrants and poor people were subject to. He saw
how important it was to be trusted by someone—anyone—
who would extend money with the only collateral being the
promise to pay it back. That is called a loan, not a handout!
And it can become the first rung in the ladder of individual
success and prosperity. Giannini decided that such loans would
be his work, and people needing such loans his customers.

That was his key decision #1—he identified his "unique

business proposition" and his target market. His key decision #2—go where the customers are. Let me explain; this will take a little longer.

Amadeo Pietro Giannini was born in San Jose, California, in 1870, one of three children of Italian immigrant parents, Luigi and Virginia. Luigi had come to California to work the Gold Rush, but eventually bought a forty-acre farm and began growing fruits and vegetables. In 1877, he was murdered in a dispute over an employee's pay. Virginia continued in the produce trade and, when she remarried, her new husband expanded the business, called L. Scatena & Co. A.P., a teenager by then, dropped out of school and went to work for his stepfather. Eventually, he took over the business and became one of the most successful wholesale produce brokers in the Santa Clara Valley.

When he was thirty-one and married, A.P. sold his position in L. Scatena to his employees and retired comfortably, spending his time managing his late father-in-law's estate. This led to a position on the board of directors of the Columbus Savings and Loan, one of the estate's holdings. There, he began to formulate and try to put into practice his ideas on lending to "regular" people. But that bank was not receptive, so he began his own, called the Bank of Italy, in 1904 in a saloon in the North Beach section (still known today as the Italian section) of San Francisco. He attracted customers—"working people to buy houses and open businesses"—and quickly earned the nickname "the little fellow's banker." After only one year, the bank had deposits of $700,000 (around $17 million in today's world). Things were looking good for A.P.

Today, we would characterize what A.P. was doing as close to . . . bootstrapping, micro-lending, micro-finance. The practice is very common in third-world countries where entrepreneurs are trying to start from the ground up, and they seek financing from motivated individuals (not banks). Credit unions, first developed in Europe in the mid-nineteenth century, serve a similar purpose by aligning individuals of similar interests, employment, financial need, geography and other factors. The first American credit union was started in 1909 in New Hampshire, where laborers faced the same kind of discrimination from banks that Giannini experienced in San Francisco. Thanks to state and federal legislation in the '30s, the credit union movement spread throughout the country. In 2016, there were almost 6,000 credit unions in the US with 104 million individual members; the supervising federal agency is the National Credit Union Administration.

And then came the historic San Francisco earthquake early one April morning in 1906 and the subsequent several days of fire. Another thirty years would pass before the Richter scale was developed, but this earthquake has been estimated at 7.9. It was characterized as "extreme" and shook the ground from Oregon to Los Angeles and across Nevada. What was not leveled instantly in the city (and its environs) by the temblor and its aftershocks, was soon engulfed by flames that also threatened the rest of the city. Eighty percent of San Francisco lay in complete ruin.

You know the adage, "It's better to be lucky than smart"? Well, A.P. was both in the hours after 5:12 A.M. on April 18, 1906. Most important, he and his family survived the quake. His home, in then-rural San Mateo south of the city, was never imperiled by fire. Obviously, not everyone shared this luck or providence or fate. But A.P. was also smart. He made key decision #2.

★   ★   ★

He immediately left his home and hurried to his bank in North Beach, some twenty miles away. It was still very early in the morning. Imagine the scenes of devastation he encountered! He emptied his bank vault and hid the money in a truck filled with garbage (some sources say produce). Then he fled to safety. As soon as the aftershocks and the flames had settled down and it was somewhat safe to come back to the ruined city, A.P. set up an outdoor bank outside of his ruined one. He placed a wooden board atop two barrels as a makeshift counter—and began giving out money "on a face and a signature." His only condition was that the recipient had to promise to use it to rebuild. Lore has it that every single dollar was repaid.

No other bankers did what A.P. did. In some cases, their bank buildings were so wrecked that the vaults were unreachable. In other cases, the extreme heat from the fire prevented the vaults, even though not breached or damaged, from being opened. And who knew what the condition of the contents would be? Currency and stock certificates surely would have disintegrated. Basically, though, these competitors were not as entrepreneurial or daring as "the little fellow's banker" was. They waited . . . for the right time, for order to be restored in the city, for organized plans to be agreed to, for the hierarchy to decide what to do, for many reasons. Not being part of "the establishment," A.P. was not included in the meetings the mayor convened to deal with the disaster. A.P. was free to act, as he had before and would continue to, according to his own intuition and judgment.

With these two iconoclastic decisions—his focus on the "small" customer and his informal branch bank that met the people where they were—A.P. built the foundation of the consumer banking culture we know today. He changed the face of finance and therefore the world.

The attitudes that Giannini observed in the banking business in 1906 were not unique to San Francisco. Banks had existed from the very founding of this country. The first ones were chartered in New England and operated as commercial lenders, catering to individuals and small businesses. Farther to the south, investment banks rose up in New York City and Philadelphia. Many of these were linked to European financial houses, some through German-Jewish immigrant roots and others—so-called "Yankee houses"—connected to the expatriate American banking community in London. Financing wars, working with the government, and helping businesses dreamed up by entrepreneurs get off the ground, these banks were not always welcoming to working-class folk and were often accused of insider lending.

While legislation aimed at regulating and organizing development tried to keep apace (as it does today), banking seemed to want it two ways. On the one hand, the very rapid growth and industrialization of the country fostered a "wild West" atmosphere of opportunity. On the other hand, a highly privileged and stratified scene arose during the so-called Gilded Age of the latter half of the nineteenth century. And keep in mind that New Englanders and New Yorkers "back East" had a head start over California in "the business of business." "The First Bank of the United States" (that actually was its name) opened in Philadelphia in 1791. California did not really open until the Gold Rush of 1849. In so many ways, A. P. Giannini was an upstart.

As we all know, San Francisco rebuilt. And then some. The importance of A.P. and his Bank of Italy in that process cannot be overstated. Through his subsequent related ventures, until his death in 1949, A.P. spread his vision of serving the "regular" financial customer throughout the state of California and into the rest of the United States and internationally. He seemed not to forget his roots. He addressed the complex needs of iconic California industries such as wine- and moviemaking as adroitly as he did the humble needs of the immigrant working people who came to that first branch in North Beach.

His bank was the major investor behind that most romantic of structures, in San Francisco and the world, the Golden Gate Bridge. And his eponymous foundation focuses on research to treat human disease.

A.P. merged his Bank of Italy with Los Angeles-based Bank of America in 1928 to better facilitate his expansion plans (including adopting the more strategic name). Weathering the Great Depression and continuing to thrive, the Bank of America became the largest commercial bank in the US (largest branch system, too). The bank was acquired by NationsBank in 1998, and the entire entity is now the second largest bank in the country and in the top ten in the world. A.P. also founded Transamerica (in San Francisco, now worldwide) in 1930 as an insurance and financial services holding company

What lessons on decision-making can we take from A.P.? I'll start with these four:

1. Remember your roots and the values you learned and apply them throughout your life.

2. Be firm and brave. Bucking the banking trends of his time, A.P. showed conviction, spunk, and spine. And don't forget to be prompt and timely. When you know what you are going to do, go for it.

3. Be proud of your unique ideas and decisions, because no one else has them. Be confident in testing their worthiness with others. Like many of the leaders profiled in this book, A.P. knew when and how to ask for advice. The key attribute of an A.P. advisor? Someone "whose judgment I respect," he said. Works for me.

4. Be focused on acting on the main chance, and do not obsess on perfection to the point of losing your opportunity. Maybe you'll just get there a little more slowly. As someone else said "The perfect is the enemy of the good." As for the rest, let's go right to the source.

What did A. P. Giannini himself say?

1. "It's no use, however, to decide what's going to happen unless you have your convictions. Many a brilliant idea has been lost because the man who dreamed it lacked the spunk, or the spine, to put it across."

2. "Don't dawdle. When you have a purpose in hand, go after it and achieve it as promptly and efficiently as you can. I have never believed in beating around the bush."

3. "When you have ideas different from others, you are never broke, so long as the ideas are good. When I have an idea, I consider it from all sides—the good and the bad, the black and white of it. Then I go to someone whose judgment I respect and let him punch holes in it. If the worst he can say has still some good in it, then I go ahead."

4. "It doesn't matter if you don't always hit the exact bull's eye. The other rings in the target score points too."

9

HENRY FORD

> Any decision you make isn't worth a tinker's damn
> until you have formed the habit of making it and
> keeping it.
> —HENRY FORD

IMAGINE THAT this is your situation:

Your young company is a raging success. Its product, a simple one that can be produced easily because of a manufacturing process that you invented, is wildly popular.

Then imagine that this is your problem:

You have to replace your workers three or four times a year. Your great manufacturing process is driving your employees away. They can't tolerate it!

What would you do?

Anyone who runs a business knows that a high employee turnover rate is . . . well, bad. The ability to attract and retain employees is key to longevity and success. How long can a business survive if its entire workforce turns over three or four times a year?

As someone who has run his own business for over twenty-five years, I have many thoughts on this question. If my business had such a high employee turnover rate, do you think it would occur to me to double my employees' wages?

That's what this particular business owner did. His name is Henry Ford, and we all know what the Ford Motor Company is. Maybe you bought one of the 2.5 million vehicles that Ford sold in the US last year.

Let me set the scene, and then talk about the decision Ford

made to save his company—a business decision that *Fortune* magazine said is the "greatest" of all time.

Henry Ford founded his company in 1903 to manufacture vehicles for the "common man." The automobile itself had already been invented—the adage "success has many fathers, but failure is an orphan" comes to mind, as there are several "fathers" of the first car (in fact, it was probably the German Karl Benz in 1885 or so).

But in 1903, automobiles were an elite product. Only the rich could afford them. They were hand-built, often to personal specifications. They were also very heavy, as they had to withstand the rigors of mostly unpaved roads used by the horse-and-wagon mode of transportation.

Though his was not the only automobile company, Henry Ford had some key early insights. He simplified the design and construction of the automobile, narrowed the choices available ("any color you want, so long as it's black") and marketed it toward what we would today call the "down market." And as the American road system improved because more people were driving cars, the cars themselves could become lighter, a fact that Ford took advantage of.

In 1913, Ford took a huge leap forward. He abandoned the traditional hand-building process that involved each worker performing a number of different tasks to put a car together. That was inefficient! Especially when demand for Ford's products was ballooning—workers could not work fast enough.

Instead of having the car-in-process stay in one place on the factory floor, with workers walking around to different locations to get what they needed and then walking back to the car, Ford instituted the "assembly line." The car-in-process would be dragged or pushed or otherwise conveyed along a line. Workers would stay in one place, performing one task. Upon completion, the car would move along to the next group of workers, who would perform another task.

Revolutionary! More efficient! And, at first, easier on the workers. But workers began to lose the sense that an entire car was emerging under their hands. Doing the same task over and over was not as satisfying. And as assembly-line technology improved, so too did its speed, which soon became a source of great stress. The workers could hardly keep up. And thus was born the problem of high employee turnover. Almost as soon as they learned what to do on the job, workers decided that they did not want the job.

Only a year after Ford's revolutionary invention, it was obvious that the assembly line had a huge unforeseen downside. Ford's company was in a precarious position. The cost of finding and retraining workers was becoming crippling. The efficiency that was the promise of the assembly line could not be sustained. Both revenues and profits were beginning to decline.

It's interesting to me that Ford's solution was not to change the nature of the assembly line. As I noted at the very beginning of this chapter, Henry Ford both made and kept to his decisions. We have seen this trait in other key decision-makers. Ford believed in his invention.

But his invention depended on human beings, not robots (remember, this was 1914). If Ford's employees were not thriving, then he would have to change the conditions under which they worked. Make the conditions more attractive. Raising pay was the obvious first step.

"The $5 Day" came at a time when most assembly line workers were making about $2.50 a day. This wage-doubling was not arbitrary. Ford and his advisors determined that anything less would not be an effective incentive, and anything more would begin to depress profits. An additional $2.50 was the sweet spot. A related initiative was the three-shift-per-day schedule (rather than two), which opened up more actual jobs.

The "$5 Day" not only solved Ford's immediate problem. Deceptively simple, his decision also sowed the seeds of the culture of consumerism that pervades, even defines, our lives today. For good or ill. That's why *Fortune*'s editors named it as the ultimate in their 2012 book *The Greatest Business Decisions of All Time*. Earning $5 a day, Ford's workers could finally afford to buy that Model T they were making.

> The $5 Day was only the first of many groundbreaking employee-socialization efforts (mostly good, but at the same time controversial) that Ford instituted. These were grounded in a combination of his personal beliefs and his determination to run a thriving business. For example, the "Socialization Department" sent examiners into employees' homes to observe, evaluate and "help"; better home life, better employees. The Ford "English Department" existed to teach new immigrant workers the language of their new land. Not only was this a path to citizenship, it also made communication on the factory floor more efficient and less dangerous; the Tower of Babel has no place on the assembly line.

Henry Ford was nothing if not a visionary, iconoclastic, and decisive businessman. Even early in his career, he possessed those qualities, and his reputation only grew throughout his lifetime. Today, seventy-two years after the founder's retirement and seventy years after his death, Ford is one of the great companies of our time.

Do you think Henry Ford, as astute as he was, had any inkling what his 1914 decision to double his workers' wages—in today's parlance, to pay his workers a living wage—would mean?

★   ★   ★

Here are the top lessons I take from Henry Ford's $5 Day decision that can apply to us:

1. Your employees need to be rewarded and feel rewarded. They need the tangibility of proper compensation and the intangibility of satisfaction. All people need to be valued.

2. Life and business are both constantly moving. You need to monitor and be ready to adjust.

3. No matter how important you or your organization is, you need to show compassion and to listen to and mentor those around you.

4. Effects of decisions are sometimes better appreciated in hindsight. Sometimes effects are what has been hoped for, but sometimes there are "unintended consequences."

5. You don't have to be a corporate CEO to benefit from Ford's example. He carefully studied the problems inherent in the automobile-manufacturing process as well as the ramifications of various ways to address the problems. Then, he made his decisions and quickly implemented them.

6. Zero in on your biggest problem. Focus on the real obstacles before you, not the distractions.

7. Honor tradition but do not be hidebound to it.

8. Understand the importance of people and the impact of your decision on them. Then, act accordingly.

9. Always think of the result or payoff of your decision so that you can use that decision to motivate yourself and others.

10

HOWARD JOHNSON

Today's standardization . . . is the necessary
foundation on which tomorrow's improvements
will be based.
—HENRY FORD

I DON'T KNOW whether Henry Ford (1863–1947) and Howard
Johnson (1897–1972) ever met. But I think they were kindred
spirits.

As you recall from the preceding chapter, Henry Ford invented the "assembly line" in 1913 to make it easier for his
Detroit company to make Model Ts and Model As. With a
standardized process in place, his already successful business
became even more so and eventually the entire manufacturing
industry was revolutionized.

Some twenty-two years later, Howard Johnson began selling his name and a proven "package" of recipes and procedures
as a way to expand his small restaurant business near Boston.
With new individual operators following his standards in their
own small businesses all named "Howard Johnson's," he gained
the necessary foothold for profitable growth. The concept of
"franchising" revolutionized the entire hospitality industry
and became commonplace in other industries as well.

Ford's customers could count on the cars rolling off Detroit's
assembly lines being "any color they want, so long as it's black."
(That's one of the sayings attributed to Henry Ford about the
attention he paid to customer preferences; he may have also
said, "If I had asked people what they wanted, they would have
said faster horses.") As for Howard Johnson's customers, once

they spotted those orange roofs and turquoise accents and the Simple Simon icon, they started salivating for clam strips, clam chowder, and "frankforts" (never called "hot dogs").

Did Howard Johnson decide to pursue franchising for any reason other than to solve an immediate problem? Did he know what a significant mark he would make in the hospitality industry (once he added motels and commissaries to his roadside restaurants, familiarly known as HoJo's)? Could he see ahead that far? Maybe selling his first franchise was just a plain old one-off survival tactic that looks grander in hindsight. We've all made decisions like that.

In any event, Johnson's decision came just at the time when people were "taking to the road" in their new Fords and Chevys and Buicks. As American travelers began routinely venturing farther and farther from home on the new parkways and turnpikes of the 1930s and '40s and the new interstates of the 1950s, they needed places to eat and sleep along the way. Sure, there had always been local eateries and inns, but maybe you were nervous about their quality. Once Johnson set "the standard," you knew what you were getting. That concept applied to any of 1,000 locations, primarily in the Northeast, Mid-Atlantic and Midwest states, where the company did business at its peak.

The decision-making lesson here is to do your research and be aware of the external conditions in which you're operating. And take advantage of them to serve your particular goals. You need as much information as possible. Good decisions are seldom made because of ignorance or wishful thinking. As you know from your own lives, few decisions stand alone; they lead to more and more. Even more reason to have your initial decisions be strong ones.

As a youngster, I counted on HoJo's clam strips when my parents loaded me and my siblings into the Buick and went motoring around in Connecticut and, later, Ohio. I have friends who tell me that going to their hometown HoJo's for birthdays and other family events was where they learned how to behave in a restaurant. Menus with choices! Waitresses! Table service! And all those flavors of ice cream to choose from—talk about difficult decisions!

Nostalgia aside, why was Johnson's franchising decision so important? Because the concept he pioneered transformed the way Americans—and people in the rest of the world— eat when they are not at home. The food-franchise industry is much more complex than it was in Johnson's time, but as a whole, it accounts for more than $350 billion in annual revenue, or about 2 percent of American GNP. The entire American restaurant industry is about $800 billion. Worldwide, the industry is worth about $3 trillion.

Incidentally, the food franchise that most people can name without even thinking—McDonald's—was founded as a company in 1940 and first franchised in 1953. Part of its ascendency can be attributed to its success in winning turnpike/interstate rest-stop contracts away from Howard Johnson's, which previously had a lock on the major roadways in New England, New Jersey, and Pennsylvania. American travelers' eating habits were changing in a way that McDonald's was better suited to address—think "fast food" consumed in the car while driving.

Howard Deering Johnson's early life was marked by setbacks, tough experiences, and outright failure. He was born in Boston in 1897, and his formal education never went beyond the eighth grade because he had to quit and work in his father's cigar store. Like many of his peers, he went off to Europe to serve in World War I. After he safely returned, he tried various ways to pay off the family's debts after his father died, but in 1924, he went into bankruptcy owing $10,000.

Even so, the next year he began a lifelong rebound. In 1925, he was able to borrow—and soon pay back—$2,000 to buy a pharmacy in Quincy, about twelve miles from Boston. The pharmacy had a soda fountain, which became the foundation of his empire. And even though, just like everyone else and every other business, he was hammered by the 1929 Stock Market Crash, the Great Depression, and the Second World War, he and his company adjusted and persevered.

Let's go back to that pharmacy in Quincy. While overall sales were pretty good, the pharmacy's best feature was its soda fountain and thus its ice cream. Johnson got the idea that if he improved the quality of the ice cream, he would sell more of it. So, he decided on three innovations. First, he tweaked a new recipe featuring better ingredients and more butterfat. Second, selling from pushcarts, he went directly to customers rather than waiting for them to come to him. (Remember A.P. Giannini's key decision #2?) And third, he developed more flavors than the usual vanilla-chocolate-strawberry trio—twenty-eight of them, in fact. Apparently, Johnson never forgot what brought him his first success—after retiring in 1959, he would be driven around in a Cadillac with license plates reading "HJ-28."

For decision-makers like you and me, the internal environment is as important as the external environment. You know that internal environment better than anyone. What are your strengths, and what are your weaknesses? What are your dreams, and what's just wishful thinking? Will your decision, once it's made, stand on a strong foundation? Howard Johnson, the man, loved to eat ice cream. Those three key decisions he made—quality, delivery system, and choice—persuaded a lot of other people to love his ice cream, too, and go to his restaurants to get it.

Ice cream pushcarts led to roadside and beachside stands. The soda fountain added hamburgers and hot dogs (later called "frankforts") to its offerings, and early in 1929 an actual sit-down, table-service restaurant with an expanded menu based on Johnson's own recipes. But Johnson could not expand any further on his own while keeping his quality high and costs under control. So, in 1935, he took on a partner, began franchising and grew what became, in its heyday in the 1950s, the country's largest restaurant chain. Johnson founded strong supporting businesses as well—motels, food commissaries to supply HoJo's as well as various customer institutions such as supermarket frozen food.

There are so many colorful bits to Johnson's story. One is his decision to hire Jacques Pépin into, basically, his management-training program. We all recognize Pépin for the long and multi-faceted career he built for himself in the world of food. As a young man who already had won many accolades as a chef in France, Pépin came to the U.S. in 1959 and was cooking at one of New York's finest French restaurants, Le Pavillon, one of Johnson's favorites.

Attuned as always to the need for quality in his own company (remember one of those early ice cream lessons—quality ingredients), Johnson first assigned Pépin to work in his huge central commissary in Queens, New York. Someone (lots of someones) had to make all that clam chowder to supply all those restaurants.

Centralization was one of the main tenets of Johnson's devotion to standardization, franchising, and growth, but quality is very hard to maintain in such a setting. Pépin worked for Johnson for ten years (including much time spent on recipe development) and wrote fondly of the entire experience. (Pierre Franey, another culinary luminary who went on to a popular career, was a friend of Pépin's and also worked at that same commissary.)

The lesson here for me, making decisions daily to keep my own firm successful, is to always be attuned to what will strengthen your initial decision. In Johnson's case, one of the factors was having the right people. Indeed, one of my own first decisions, when I founded the Dilenschneider Group in 1991, was, "Who should I bring on board who has the skills I need to help carry out my mission?"

As Johnson honed his franchising concept, more and more he needed people to "buy in" (literally) with him. From personal experience, I think that must have been hard for him, as both his early and his continued success depended on him being in personal control of so many variables. (The handbook of procedures was called "The Howard Johnson Bible.") But I sense that he was also acutely aware of basic human motivations, including self-worth and self-determination. He once told an interviewer, "This is what I like best—help a good man to make a go of it himself."

The world of franchised or "chain" restaurants has changed immensely since the heyday of the HoJo's small regional U.S. empire, but in many ways that Johnson himself would have recognized. He certainly knew of McDonald's and Burger King, both of which were lively young upstarts in his time. What are those iconic food destinations—and Wendy's, founded after Johnson died, but highly standardized, fully national and international versions of their long-gone founders' visions? They often offer special menu items geared to certain regions, but no one is "freelancing" those recipes in the kitchen. And no one is freelancing the recognizable signage and building design elements that pull hungry customers in for the kind of hamburger they have come to expect. All of these eateries, and their fast-food cousins, gained their traction by aggressively capitalizing on one of Johnson's key principles—be where the people are. For HoJo's, that meant the newly developing American road system of the 1930s and '40s; McDonald's, the rest stops along the newly developing interstate highway systems of the 1950s. What about hospitals, airports, shopping centers, college cafeterias? And why be limited to the United States?

Just two examples of the new world of quite specific eating places aimed at the masses are provided by the founders of Chipotle (which "reinvented" fast food, and has 2,408 outlets, all but about thirty in the US; HoJo's totaled a thousand) and The Cheesecake Factory (seventh-largest American chain; it has no franchisees). These founders remain active in their publicly traded companies.

It's fun to imagine how Howard Johnson himself would

have made decisions about international operations or tweaking the frankfort or being listed on a stock exchange (HoJo's went public two years after his retirement). It's sobering to think about the decisions he would have had to make if his restaurant empire had faced the trials of highly publicized cases of food poisoning.

And I'll bet that Howard Johnson, who loved fine dining as much as he did those iconic twenty-eight ice cream flavors, would have been great friends with today's big-city "name" restaurateurs such as Danny Meyer and David Barber and Roy Yamaguchi. A man willing to take a chance, he would have applauded the legions of new regional and ethnic chefs on the way up in the industry. All of these innovators have found their own ways to communicate, through their restaurants, their unique views of food and dining.

And who knows what Howard Johnson, with his roots in the pre-mass-media world and whose protégé Jacques Pépin broke some TV ground, would think of such televised empires as "Top Chef," "Chopped," "Barefoot Contessa" and "Cupcake Wars"? Or internet-based delivery options? Can't get off the couch and go to the restaurant? No longer are you limited to calling up your favorite local joint and ordering in some pizza or chow mein. Go to a website, follow the directions (including providing your credit card info) and chose from an ever-growing but curated list of local restaurants whose food will effortlessly arrive at your front door. (Actually, some of these sites allow you to make an old-fashioned phone call.) I think Johnson would have lobbied to make HoJo's one of the website options. Though Johnson might have been puzzled to read a testimonial I found on the Grubhub.com home page: "Made my first Grubhub order today. So great to be able to order food and not have to talk to anyone." What, no personal connection? But hey, the customer—the diner—is always right.

What place did luck take in Johnson's history? Be reminded of two adages: "Better to be lucky than smart" and "Luck is the residue of hard work." Was it through luck or brains or hard work that Johnson's first sit-down restaurant, in Quincy, was located near a theatre that ran a five-hour-long banned-in-Boston play with an intermission at dinner time? All those cultured Bostonians who ventured out to the hinterlands in late 1929 to see Eugene O'Neill's play *Strange Interlude* went home raving about where they had had dinner. Today's version of Yelp, maybe. We all know how effective word-of-mouth recommendations are.

For a decision-maker, the message seems clear. Be prepared to react to circumstances, not like an out-of-control weathervane, but like a hunter in the woods, following the footprints, scat, and other signs in front of you. Once Johnson realized that those theatre-goers were a "captive audience," he had every cook, waiter, and waitress stay on duty—no time off during the run of the play.

The very last HoJo's closed early in 2017. There are no vestiges of the restaurant and commissary empire except in people's memories and an organized fan group. There had been a time when only the Army fed more people in a day than Howard Johnson's businesses did. The name "Howard Johnson's" as a hotel lives on in the archives of Wyndham Worldwide, which bought it from the Marriott Corporation. If you ever see a Simple Simon sign or statuette in a vintage shop, grab it. And think about how Johnson's one-foot-in-front-of-the-other series of decisions shaped an industry that changed the eating habits of America, and therefore the world.

I still miss those clam strips.

Here are the major decision-making lessons from Howard Johnson's story:

    1. Create a vision—where do you want to go and focus everything you have on it.

    2. Build your decisions on what you know. One step at a time. At the same time, take a chance.

3. Do your homework. What external conditions do you need to pay attention to? What are your own "internal" conditions?

4. You will not be able to foresee all or even many of the results of your decisions. As those results become apparent, and external/internal conditions change, be prepared to make new decisions.

5. Assume that whatever the future of your decisions, it will take many steps to get to the final results. Do not lose heart.

6. Know everything you can about the needs and desires of the people who will be affected by your decisions or who will need to carry out your decisions.

7. Think quality and top-of-the-line, always, as the desired result of your decisions.

8. Look around corners for problems and what might impede your progress and address it, if possible, before it happens.

PART THREE
Science

11

ALEXANDER FLEMING, LOUIS PASTEUR, IGNAZ SEMMELWEIS

> Biologists practice evidence-based decision-making.
> —LOUIS PASTEUR

COUNT ME AMONG THOSE who apparently didn't get the "science gene." In my case, the Bunsen burner in my high school lab did me in. I know many people who, faced with dissecting a rubbery dead frog, gave the scalpel back to the biology teacher and decided to major in English Lit.

But fortunately for all of us, there are many people who, genetically endowed or not, live and work in the land of science.

Two of those people were Louis Pasteur and Alexander Fleming. Their medical discoveries continue to shape the course of human life. Their biographies are well-known. Both had long and illustrious careers based, upon my knowledge of the demands of any career, on constant decision-making. And that's why they are in this book. As is a third man, Ignaz Semmelweis, less well-known but equally vital.

Vaccinations (Pasteur) and antibiotics (Fleming)—every single reader of this book has been given multiples of these once-revolutionary substances. They are an inescapable part of modern life and responsible for myriad public-health benefits. The use of vaccines has nearly eradicated many dreaded diseases and lessened the effects of many, many others. Estimates of the lives saved by antibiotics top 200,000,000.

Certainly, there are nay-sayers about both medicines, but their power makes Pasteur's and Fleming's decisions all the more admirable, in my view. As for Semmelweis and his groundbreaking work as a physician, developing antiseptic practices, don't you wash your hands a lot? Aren't we all in favor of proper medical hygiene?

From the beginning of time to this very morning, human beings have been trying to cure human ailments. Even two centuries ago, these efforts were aimed largely at ameliorating symptoms—*preventing* ailments in the first place seemed almost beyond reach. While anyone could see that there was an obvious cause-and-effect between infection and disease, "spontaneous generation" was the closest scientists could come to an explanation.

Louis Pasteur was the French chemist and biologist whose work in the mid-late 1800s disproved "spontaneous generation" and proved the "germ theory": disease is caused by microscopic organisms that once identified, can be eliminated by vaccinations. Even as I write them, these words sound so clinical. Pasteur intrigues me not only for his discovery, but because of a couple of reckless decisions he made along the way to proving the viability of the rabies vaccination in particular.

Alexander Fleming attracts for an opposite reason— doggedness rather than recklessness. Working in a world that now accepted "germ theory," this physician constantly sought new ways to kill germs. But he didn't keep the neatest laboratory in early twentieth century Scotland (some might even have said it was downright sloppy). A lapse in procedure should have led him to discard that Petri dish with the funny new mold growing on it. But Fleming decided to investigate the mold, which led to the discovery of penicillin. A modest man, I think, Fleming mused at one point, "I certainly didn't plan to . . . but I suppose that was exactly what I did."

The first decision that any scientist makes is to pursue an idea. If experiment and other research show that the idea has promise, the decision is made to continue to pursue it. And this process plays out—sometimes over the course of many years, and through many twists and turns. Decision after decision.

As I think about Pasteur and Fleming, I can visualize a baton of sorts being passed between the two men. Their lifetimes spanned 133 years of almost incredible breakthroughs by many, many scientists. Pasteur was born in 1822 and died in 1895; his major discovery/decision took place in 1885. Fleming was born in 1881 and died in 1955. His major discovery/decision unfolded between 1921 and 1928. And their baton—the work done on vaccinations and antibiotics by countless others—continues its journey.

To oversimplify what happened in 1885, Pasteur unilaterally decided to administer his newly discovered rabies vaccine twice to humans, after having had some qualified success with treating rabid dogs. These two "human trials" took place without proper documentation and in settings of secrecy because, being "only" a chemist/biologist and not a physician, he was not authorized to treat humans. One of Pasteur's patients then disappeared, possibly after being cured but this is not certain, and the other died almost immediately. It was the third administration—properly and publicly documented—that was successful. And, as they say, the rest is history.

Was this the work of a reckless man, a prideful man, or a supremely confident man who believed firmly in his work? After all, Pasteur was already widely acclaimed for having "saved" two of France's key industries—wine in 1865 (with the process that became known as "pasteurization") and silk in 1868.

A generation later, Alexander Fleming made a decision that

was almost the opposite of Pasteur's in its seeming innocuousness. Deep into the process of investigating what caused the common cold, one day in 1921 Fleming had blown his nose and put the secretions onto a slide. The slide got somehow put aside in Fleming's admittedly disorganized lab.

When he found the slide again several weeks later, Fleming probably should have discarded it because who knows what else was now on it besides his mucus. But he could see that the mucus had prevented the growth of any germs. Fleming decided to pursue that slender thread to its eventual conclusion a decade later, the discovery of penicillium mold, the basis for the drug penicillin. Was he aware of the saying attributed to Pasteur, that "chance favors the prepared mind"? Regardless, as was the case with Pasteur and rabies, the rest is history.

In presenting these brief accounts of very complex people and endeavors, I have perhaps unavoidably given you the impression that these notable decision-makers Pasteur and Fleming worked in isolation. In fact, the opposite is true. Both men were steeped in a milieu that I would call "collegial competition" with scientific and medical discoveries being made right and left, with hordes of people feverishly—so to speak—toiling away at so many new possibilities, racing to bring research to reality. Think about Ernst Chain, Marie Curie, Howard Florey, Edward Jenner, Robert Koch, Charles Laveran, Joseph Lister, Florence Nightingale, and Jonas Salk among so many others.

Many of us have the image of scientists working in solitude, lonely in their labs. And while individual focus is the foundation, there is really no such thing as privacy in science. It is a communal effort. It may not always be collegial, but it features groups.

This resonates with me. Earlier, I mentioned that the Bunsen burner had turned me away from science. Actually, I might have enjoyed a career in science, because the combination of individual and communal work is a very satisfying part of the career I did pursue.

And thinking about all this has given me some insight, I think, into Pasteur and Fleming. They did not toil in obscurity. In the course of their careers, they practiced their own brand of public relations, even if that's not what they called it. But consider. They published, they defended their work publicly, they attracted funding, they recruited other colleagues and researchers, they held responsible positions in major institutions and—in Pasteur's case—founded one that flourishes globally to this day, the Pasteur Institute.

Depending on the nature of your "decision," you may want to do one or more of these things, too. They are not out of your reach.

Additionally, Pasteur and Fleming seem to me to have been very charismatic and personable men. They were leaders. They attracted others to work with them. They must have inspired trust. They cared deeply about people, both their loved ones and all those who suffer, known or not. They had deep sorrows in their lives, including deaths of children (in Pasteur's case) and a brother (Fleming's) from diseases that their discoveries could have helped if the timing had been different.

Questions of visibility, communication, and personal charisma bring me to another pioneer in the brave new world of germ theory—Ignaz Semmelweis, who bucked the mid-nineteenth century medical power structure. Though I'll bet you've never heard of him, he is probably responsible for the fact that we wash our hands so often.

Semmelweis was born in 1818 and died in 1865. Educated in Hungary and Austria, he was practicing medicine at the Vienna General Hospital in 1847, the time of his great discovery/decision. Spontaneous generation was beginning to be supplanted by germ theory.

Semmelweis belongs in this book because he decided to

pay attention to "childbed (puerperal) fever," which of course struck only women after childbirth and was almost invariably and horribly fatal. (I'll get to the hand-washing.) Mothers, in fact, had identified the crux of the "childbed fever" problem long before doctors (generally men) did.

Before the mid-nineteenth century, most babies were born at home with midwives (generally women) attending mother and child. Infection and risks of all kinds were constant threats, but doctors were normally called in only for emergencies. As "health care" institutions began to develop, birthing moved out of the home and, more and more, doctors supplanted midwives. And that's when Semmelweis noticed, as did new and prospective mothers, that there was a connection between childbed fever (and mothers dying) and babies born with a doctor's help versus a midwife's.

I've given you a red herring here. What's relevant is not the gender of the doctor or the midwife, but the fact that doctors almost always came to the maternity ward directly from . . . the morgue, where they performed autopsies and . . . did not wash their hands. Our modern minds reel at the implications of this unsanitary practice, but in the mid-nineteenth century when "germs" was a new concept, that's the way it was. Midwives were in the maternity ward solely to attend to their patients, and did not have the "opportunity" to carry so many germs so easily.

In 1847, when Semmelweis decided to pursue the connection that was so clear to him, he encountered what we would now call "pushback." His solution—that doctors wash up between studying the dead and attending to the living—was so simple and elegant, yet it criticized those who held the power in the practice of medicine. Doctors (male) were superior, while midwives and mothers (women) were inferior.

The fact is that some of Semmelweis's personal characteristics may have also hindered the adoption of his discovery. He was not an especially collegial or engaging fellow. He didn't seem to care how others perceived him and he didn't like to spend time communicating with peers in the medical community. He did not broadcast his discovery. Did he decide not to override these not-exactly-helpful foibles, or was he incapable of change? (By the way, Louis Pasteur was one of the scientists who was independently seeking an answer to the problem of childbed fever; just imagine if the two men had been able to combine forces.)

Regardless of who got the credit, the incidence of childbed fever dropped markedly once hand-washing became more and more routine. As it was eventually obvious that the practice had many other benefits in the hospital and every other setting (think: restaurant kitchens!), hand-washing is now second nature to all of us. And it's evolving! Recently, I read a news story reporting that it doesn't matter if you use hot or cold water—just use lots of soap and don't stop lathering until you count to ten.

Have you ever made a decision that you, and others, thought was reckless, dangerous, foolish, ill-advised, silly? Were the stakes as high—human life—as they were for Louis Pasteur, Alexander Fleming, and Ignaz Semmelweis? Even if not, there is so much to learn from these men and their decisions:

1. If you want to make a difference, identify a problem and decide to solve it.

2. Always involve others and ask advice. You do not have to take it. But if you do not ask you will never get it.

3. Seek out many ways to solve the problem, knowing that most of what you identify will not work. This means you must address the phenomenon of discouragement.

4. When you try something that doesn't work, don't give up. Recognize that rarely will success come your way the first time; trying again and again is critical to your success.

5. Do not be afraid to try something new, even if you do not like it at the start.

6. Be ready to take criticism, and even ridicule and derision. Think about this as part of your decision process. Rather than turning away, be prepared to develop a thick hide.

7. When your decision plays out to a positive result, be humble.

8. Give yourself time to dream. Hunches about outcomes are as important as provable evidence is, and only scientists need to worry about documenting and replicating their experiments.

9. Know what you're talking about. Pasteur, Fleming, and Semmelweis brought years of rigorous education and experiments, both successful and not.

10. Important decisions are not made in a vacuum. Read, research, and use the wisdom of the people in your circle to help inform your decision. But at the end of the day, it's your decision.

11. Weigh the consequences of not dotting every "i" and crossing every "t" along the way. What risks have you taken that might negate your decision? Is Pasteur's reputation damaged by what we now know about those previous secret administrations of the rabies vaccine?

12. Pay attention, notice things. You don't need to be sloppy like Fleming, but don't overlook what a "happy accident" can tell you.

13. Don't be enslaved to what conventional wisdom tells you is acceptable. If Semmelweis had, he would never have decided to face up to the medical power structure in which he was steeped.

14. Be honest about your personal desire for, or antipathy toward, visibility. That can affect the outcome of your decisions. The job doesn't stop when you make the decision—persuading others of its import may be key.

15. Deciding not to decide is also a decision. Because of his personality, Semmelweis was indifferent to taking certain actions that might have helped spread his discovery.

16. Seek and be thrilled with small victories. Taken together, they will add up to big results.

17. Never be satisfied. There is always more you can do.

18. Be sure to publicize—tell others—of the progress you have made. It may spur them to do still better for society.

12

MARIE CURIE

> It was an exceptional decision, as up to then no
> woman had held such a position.
> —MARIE CURIE

PERHAPS THE MOST MOMENTOUS decision Marie Curie ever
made was to accept someone else's decision.

In 1906, her husband Pierre, her beloved and respected
partner in life as well as in their ground-breaking physics and
chemistry research, had just been killed in a terrible accident
on a busy Paris street. The national and personal shock was
profound.

Three years earlier, in 1903, the Doctors Curie had been
jointly awarded the Nobel Prize for their work in the field
of radioactivity. Publicly, they were celebrities, though not
wealthy ones. Privately, they juggled the daily demands facing
all working parents. Professionally, the sky seemed the limit
in terms of the promise that lay before Pierre and Marie, for
at ages forty-seven and thirty-eight respectively, they were in
their prime as researchers. Now what?

Within two weeks of Pierre's death, which happened on
April 19, 1906, the French government asked Marie to take
over Pierre's leadership research and teaching position at the
University of Paris, a position that had been created for him
only recently. The fact that the initial request included the
words "acting chair," did not diminish the startling event. As
Marie later wrote of the government and the university, "It
was an exceptional decision" on their part.

Marie Curie was the first woman to achieve such promi-nence. And she was no "mere" widow who would enjoy a per-functory appointment to fill her husband's shoes. She was more than adequately qualified. "Acting" would soon disappear from her job description.

Marie was also deep in grief at the time, often distraught from her loss and seemingly paralyzed about how to go for-ward. Not just in scientific research, but as a mother of two young daughters, almost-eight Irene and Eve, about fourteen months. And she was buffeted by the demands of Nobel-related responsibilities and other expectations. In a journal that she kept for about a year after Pierre's fatal accident, Marie expressed the wish to join him in death. As for accepting the chair, she was almost indifferent.

But accept it she did. Marie Curie's world-changing work on radioactivity would continue.

In the twenty-eight years of the rest of Mare Curie's life and career, great richness flowed from her laboratory in Paris. Discovery after discovery about the nature of radioactiv-ity, its chemical sources, its application for both therapy and destruction—all this and more. And the achievements were not hers alone. Hundreds of scientists were employed in her lab throughout the twentieth century, including Marie's daughter, Irene, and Irene's husband and, eventually, their daughter and son-in-law, and their progeny.

Marie's lab lives on today as the cancer-focused Institute Curie, formed as a result of various alliances starting in 1909 among the University of Paris, the Institut Pasteur, the Institut du Radium, and the Curie Foundation.

Let's pause here.

Marie's life story, as you will see, is one of single-minded focus and decisiveness. But in those weeks after Pierre's death, her core qualities seemed to have disappeared. To those around her, not only did she not seem to care about taking over Pierre's position, she didn't seem to *want* to care. This is classic behavior among people who are newly bereaved or otherwise traumatized—today, we are counseled not to make any major decisions at such times.

If you put yourself in Marie's position, you can appreciate that there were lots of "official" people from the university pressuring her to say "yes." Possibly they really cared about her welfare, but also her acceptance, acquiescence, assent—call it what you will—was expedient for them. But what if you also knew that her close family also wanted her to say "yes" because they saw what her life purpose was? I think that's ultimately what Marie fell back on. She trusted these family members— her sister-confidante Bronya, Pierre's physicist brother Paul-Jacques and her widowed father-in-law Eugene, who lived with the young family and provided them with much support and stability (and was a physician, and thus anther Dr. Curie). They repaid the trust with advice that meant the best for her. Her core qualities had not disappeared, they were . . . on sabbatical. Marie returned in full force.

We should all be fortunate enough to have such advisors around us, or to be such an advisor, and not just at times of trauma. Existing relationships already built on trust can provide us with the foundation we need to make our own good decisions.

Even before the 1906 turning point, it is notable how many decisions Marie Curie had already faced down in her life, as she pursued her education and her career. Her motivation for all of her decisions was very clear—the pursuit of science.

Marie was born Marya (or Manya, as she was affectionately called as a young girl) Sklodowska in 1867 in Warsaw, Poland, as the youngest of five children. Her family occupied a comfortable place in Poland. Before Marya's birth, her mother had been the director of a top school for girls. Her father taught high school physics and math, and his many scientific instruments at home fascinated young Marya. But Poland was Russian-occupied, not an independent country. Life for traditional Poles grew tougher with every new Russian restriction—for example, speaking Polish or studying Polish history was forbidden. Being quite pro-Polish, Marya's father eventually lost his teaching job and then, through his own bad decisions, most of the family's money.

The deaths of Marya's eldest sister in 1875 and her mother in 1877 were severe blows. As was the growing realization that, no matter how well the young woman performed in her studies (first in her high school class) and how much she enjoyed them, there would be no "higher" education—the Russians forbade this for women. It is astonishing that this condition persists anywhere today, well into the twenty-first century, but Malala Yousafzai's story tells us otherwise.

A common solution to this problem was to go to another country to study, but there was little money in Marya's family for that. So she and her sister Bronya made a pact. One would go to Paris to study and the other would remain in Poland to earn money to support her, and then would go to Paris to study and be supported. Bronya went first and Marya stayed behind.

Thirsty for learning in any form, Marya began attending a secret and illegal school (called the "Floating University" because it had no fixed location). At one point she studied science at a lab "disguised" as a museum. I can only imagine how much she would enjoy today's emphasis on STEM (science, technology, engineering and mathematics) education, especially for girls and young women.

Meanwhile, the student was also the teacher. To earn money, Marya taught when she could and spent years as governess in a wealthy family. Having finally amassed enough money, she joined Bronya in Paris in 1891. She modified her name to Marie, and serious study and research and teaching became the hallmarks of her life.

In 1894, at age twenty-seven, she was introduced to Pierre Curie. A mutual friend thought that Pierre, about ten years older and equally dedicated to science and from a scientific family, would be compatible with the serious younger woman.

This was a long shot. Pierre regarded women as distractions from study and work, and Marie only wanted to study and work; no man would have distracted her. But there was an immediate intellectual spark between the two that grew into a strong bond, and then love. After a journey back to Poland (Marie always dreamed of returning to her homeland) proved that her prospects there remained dim, Marie decided to accept Pierre's proposal of marriage. Implicit was that they would work together.

In 1895, they wed. And the Curies' headlong pursuit of radioactivity began, because the so-called "X-ray" was discovered that same year. Hard to believe that the joint story was to end only eleven years later, with Pierre's death on that Paris street.

How exciting those years between 1895 and 1906 must have been for any scientist! But especially for Marie and Pierre, who were inextricably linked in a demanding personal and professional partnership. They became parents in those years, and domestic and financial concerns were frequent. But in their own lab, and in the scientific community all around them, discoveries of all kinds were continuing to come, fast and furious.

The discoveries that most fascinated Marie and Pierre started with Wilhelm Roentgen's experiments with electricity in 1895. The German physicist had produced "rays" with the mysterious ability to pass through solid materials and leave images. He called them "X rays" because he didn't know what they were, only what they did. Months later in Paris, Henri Becquerel discovered that uranium, a known element, also emitted such rays (called radiation); Marie then discovered that another known element, thorium, did the same. It is well that we remember that radiation is a naturally occurring phenomenon that we can use for good or ill.

Moving along jointly in their research (and I am obviously oversimplifying the story; science was never my strong suit), Marie and Pierre decided to analyze rocks containing more than a single element. One type of rock—a mining by-product called pitchblende made up of both uranium and thorium—emitted much more radiation than was expected. Clearly there must be an additional source. Painstaking and time-consuming distillation of close to a ton of pitchblende (in their lab!) revealed not one, but two additional sources, heretofore unidentified. Marie named the first element polonium (after her beloved country) and the second one radium.

Marie was credited with inventing the word "radiation," and in 1910 the word "curie" became the accepted measure for doses of radiation. Not to be confused with the "Curie temperature" or the "Curie point," used in the study of magnetism and named for Pierre (whose doctorate was in magnetism).

Marie's acceptance of her pioneering appointment in 1906 was neither the first nor the last time she broke male precedent. She was the first woman in Europe to earn a Ph.D. in science (in 1903). She was the first woman to teach (her subject: physics) at the prestigious Ecole Normale Superieure de Sevres, starting in 1900. The 1903 Nobel for physics, though awarded jointly, was the first-ever to a woman. Her second Nobel, for chemistry in 1911, made her then the only two-time Nobel laureate (and in separate fields, no less); she remains the only woman to hold two awards.

The various Nobel Prizes had begun to be awarded in 1896. So in 1903, certain "rules" had yet to be really codified. The initial physics award that year was to have gone jointly to Henri Becquerel and Pierre Curie for their work on radioactivity. But Pierre objected to the omission of his total partner, Marie, and the award was adjusted to include her. (Interestingly, Becquerel got fifty percent of the monetary prize, the Curies shared the other fifty percent.) Marie won the Nobel Prize for chemistry in 1911 on the strength of her discovery of polonium and radium, and her extensive study of radium.

In 1935, Marie and Pierre's daughter Irene won the Nobel Prize for chemistry jointly with her husband Frederic Joliot; they were cited for synthesizing new radioactive elements, among their many accomplishments. In 1965, when UNICEF won the Nobel Peace Prize, Marie and Pierre's daughter Eve was that organization's director.

Even many years after her death, Marie broke precedent. In 1995, the ashes of both Pierre and Marie were taken from their original resting places and re-buried in the Pantheon, the famous Paris mausoleum. As newspaper reports noted at the time, this made "the celebrated scientist the first woman honored at the memorial dedicated to the 'great men' of France . . . a symbolic triumph for French campaigners for women's rights." Speaking at the dedication, President François Mitterrand cited the "exemplary struggle" of Marie Curie, "a woman who decided to impose her abilities in a society where abilities, intellectual exploration and public responsibility were reserved for men."

I will now describe one very, very bad decision in Marie Curie's life. And that was to overlook or ignore or not fully comprehend the obvious deleterious effects of working— literally, in a hands-on sense—with radioactive materials. The stuff can kill you. It did kill Marie, whose cause of death was a form of anemia linked to radiation exposure. Had Pierre's life not ended in that street accident, it would probably have killed him, too. Their daughter Irene, a prominent scientist in her own right, died from leukemia, the result of years of exposure to radioactive materials and a specific lab accident involving polonium—one of the elements Marie discovered.

Early in their work, both Pierre and Marie saw that handling their raw materials (which emitted a lovely glow in the lab at night) would result in burns on their fingertips that took a very long time to heal. But they did not change their habits. They (and others) chalked up their chronic exhaustion and ill health to overwork. Pierre's frequent severe aches and pains could have been arthritis or rheumatism. Marie suffered a miscarriage in the years between the births of daughters Irene in 1897 and Eve in 1904, but there are many reasons for miscarriage.

Their carelessness was shared in the larger society as well. Can you imagine adding little capsules of "Spa Radium", made by the Sparklet Soda Syphon Company to drinking water to make it, well, sparkle? How about radium-based chocolates and toothpaste? Indeed, such products existed in the 1920s. Can you imagine carrying a piece of uranium on a train trip, as Marie once did? (In a safe deposit to protect it!)

And what about the courageous effort Marie led with her daughter Irene, then a teenager, on the World War I battle-fields? Starting in 1914, in specially outfitted "petites Curie" vehicles, they X-rayed wounded soldiers right on the spot, thus making timely medical and surgical treatment more likely. They trained teams of other nurse-radiographers to do the same. This work was credited with saving one million soldiers' lives. But each X-ray resulted in radiation exposure for these brave pioneers.

We think we know better today. For example, we are carefully shielded with lead aprons if we choose to get dental X-rays. When radiation is applied for cancer treatment, customized shields are made to protect the nontreated parts of the body. Even so, the burns at the treated site are a terrible side effect. Many of us, while enjoying the convenience of cell phones and other devices that we take for granted as we use them close to our bodies, do wonder—what about radiation?

★ ★ ★

These four thoughts/lessons about decision-making are drawn from Marie Curie's example:

1. Few decisions are really made in isolation. Either they involve groups of people to carry them out, or they affect people's lives. Most of us are in the position of functioning both independently and as part of a family, a team, a department, a company, a school or a community. Therefore, let other people help you! And be willing to help them.

2. Not every decision is made under ideal circumstances. Grief, death, illness, and so many other adversities can seem to cloud our vision when decisions loom. Focus, help from others and time (don't rush, except in an emergency) are all indispensable.

3. We all make bad decisions. Let's hope that they are not as serious as the Curies' decisions around safe handling of their radioactive materials. Granted, much was unknown then, and sometimes pioneers pay a very heavy price.

4. Finally, Marie was single-minded. I have only told you about part of her life. Rest assured that the rest of her life shows that little stood in her way, and if it did, it was temporary. This gave a certain adamantine quality to her decision-making. Examine this trait for its effect on the softer sides of life—specifically, the effect on one's children and other loved ones.

13

RACHEL CARSON

> Who has made the decision that sets in motion
> these chains of poisonings, this ever-widening wave
> of death that spreads out, like ripples when a pebble
> is dropped into a still pond?
> —RACHEL CARSON

EARLY IN 1958, the *Boston Herald* published a plaintive letter from a woman who said that all of the songbirds on her farm were . . . gone. Spring that year had been . . . silent. What was happening?

That question had begun to bother a lot of other people, including Rachel Carson, who turned her search for an answer into a book.

The rest is history. The culprit killing the birds was DDT. The book was *Silent Spring,* published in 1962 and almost immediately hailed as the foundation of the worldwide modern environmental movement.

By inclination, training, and employment, Rachel Carson was a marine biologist of talent and achievement. She was also a celebrated and respected author, with a solid career and three major books to her credit, plus almost innumerable other writings. Tentatively titled "Remembrance of Life," major book #4 beckoned, but not in the way she had thought. As biographer Linda Lear writes in *Rachel Carson: Witness for Nature*:

> In fact, she had outlined precisely the theme of her
> next book. Its context, but not its philosophic intent was

altered by a series of events that enveloped Carson in the winter of 1957–58 and swept her along in an intellectual and scientific adventure beyond even her considerable powers of imagination.

The inquiry into DDT set Rachel on a new and different course, the results of which changed the world. Pre-DDT, what had been her path in life?

For Rachel, the beginning of the decade of the '50s was marked by two intertwined events. She had taken an early retirement to focus on personal priorities—which soon included many losses and a fatal cancer. I'll focus on the career event and her early years now, and talk about the losses and her cancer later in this chapter.

Having spent a secure and productive fifteen-year career with the U.S. Fish and Wildlife Service, in 1951 Rachel decided to retire. For many years she had balanced onerous family responsibilities along with her professional work in marine biology.

Somehow, though, she had found the time, her own personal time, to write many essays, articles, pamphlets, and brochures about nature and two very well reviewed books about the ocean. (The words "lyrical" and "poetry" were often used to describe her prose.) The second book had blossomed into an award-winning, serialized, bestselling blockbuster. Her third book about the ocean was underway and seemed to hold equal promise.

For the first time in her life, she was financially comfortable, even secure. She was now free to make writing about her favorite subject and caregiving of her beloveds her full-time occupation.

Let's be honest. Most of us would agree that the U.S. Fish and Wildlife Service is perhaps not the most dynamic governmental agency. And what would we conclude about a woman who would love a career there, mostly in the Publications Division?

But for Rachel Carson, fish and wildlife and publications were natural fits. Born in 1907, she had been raised as the youngest child of three on a struggling sixty-four-acre homestead in Pennsylvania in the 1910s and '20s. No electricity, no indoor plumbing, and a traveling salesman father who was often away.

Thanks to time spent playing and exploring outdoors with her mother, she was well acquainted with the pleasures and the vagaries of nature. Her mother, Maria Carson, a singer, musician, and teacher before her marriage, also encouraged Rachel to love reading and writing. The girl was publishing stories in the classic children's magazine *St. Nicholas* by the age of ten. She reveled in the tales of Beatrix Potter and Kenneth Grahame as a child, and as a teen moved on to everything from Joseph Conrad to the Romantic-era poets. She was acquainted with the work of Gene (Geneva) Stratton-Porter, a popular and influential writer, naturalist, and activist.

Rather unexpectedly, given her family's poverty, and largely because of her mother's interventions on behalf of a bright daughter, Rachel attained an excellent education. In 1929, she graduated from the prestigious Pennsylvania College for Women (now co-ed and renamed Chatham University).

There, a perceptive and prescient teacher named Mary Scott Skinker had urged her toward majoring in biology, even though it was considered a lonely and demanding field for women. Perhaps Professor Skinker knew that Rachel's great gift would lie in the intersection of science and writing. Perhaps that was Rachel's first major life decision, to major in biology instead of English.

Scholarships to the renowned Woods Hole Oceanographic Institution and to The Johns Hopkins University (where Rachel earned a master's in zoology in 1932) followed.

Rachel loved marine biology, but she never had enough money for the Ph.D.-level education that would allow her to perform original research and to become a fully-fledged Marine Biologist (with a capital M and a capital B). Quite simply, there was her family to consider at a time when the Depression reigned.

Unmarried, without a partner or family members to help, she would spend her adult years as the sole support of her widowed and, eventually, elderly and ailing mother. Maria Carson was exceedingly close to her daughter and had almost always lived with her (even bunking in the dorm some weekends at college) and who instilled in her daughter a permanent and deep love of nature. Throughout her life, Rachel also supported her infirm sister Marian. After Marian's death, she took charge of Marian's surviving daughters, one of whom died at a young age, leaving behind a little son under Rachel's care.

The combined weight of financial and family responsibilities presented twenty-nine-year-old Rachel with a series of no-choice decisions—what else could she do, but her best, to fulfill these responsibilities?

Rachel went to work, part-time at first because that's all that was available, for the Federal Bureau of Fisheries in Baltimore in 1936, writing radio scripts. Her initial work resulted in a series called "Romance Under the Waters," possibly an indication that she was no ordinary government bureaucrat.

Here's a good place to pause and think about all the decisions you and I have made at an early age. Chief among them are decisions about education, majors in college, and first jobs. Challenging in any event, but how much more so when financial pressures and family responsibilities loom large and resources are slim.

In her fifteen years at the Bureau (which became known as the U.S. Fish and Wildlife Service in 1940), Rachel held ever-increasing positions of responsibility for all publications. Examples include the "Conservation in Action" series on various national wildlife refuges. The final publication in the series was a clarion call entitled "Guarding Our National Resources." Appearing in 1946, it featured a drawing of a bald eagle on its cover, presaging Rachel's work to control the DDT whose overuse would lead to the near-extinction of our national symbol.

★   ★   ★

In 1951, as her second book about the ocean was published—to great acclaim, causing renewed attention and popularity for her previous book and ushering in some needed financial stability—Rachel left her government job, intending to focus on her family and her third marine-biology book, which would be published in 1955. It, too, would be a bestseller.

It was always evident that Rachel loved both science and writing. She possessed a unique ability to make technical information understandable and attractive to general readers, while never "dumbing it down." This one-two-three punch quickly propelled her into a unique career that enabled her both to address her family's needs and to achieve lasting global influence.

A prolific writer of letters and articles in both her professional and personal life, Rachel will always be best known for four books: *Under the Sea-Wind* (1941), *The Sea Around Us* (1951), *The Edge of the Sea* (1955) and *Silent Spring* (1962). To quote Linda Lear:

> Those four books are enough to have changed how humankind regards the living world and the future of life on this earth . . . The magnitude of Carson's impact on the public's understanding of such issues as ecology and environmental change still astonishes.

Silent Spring changed the world. It is hard to overstate the book's importance.

Silent Spring focused public attention on growing concerns about the overuse of DDT and other pesticides so that they could not be ignored. The book led to a complete reexamination of the intricate, necessary, and often exploitative relationship among humans, industry, and the natural world. It permanently changed the behavior of governments, industry, and citizens across the world. Its influence continues unabated today, almost sixty years after it appeared on the scene.

Silent Spring is considered one of the twenty-five greatest science books ever written. It has been called second only to Darwin's *Origin of Species* for its importance to science. It places near the top of every list of the twentieth century's most influential books. It is also an exquisitely beautiful work of art, using all of Rachel Carson's talents of language, imagination, and persuasion to make the complex science of chemical pesticides understandable and compelling.

The existence and use of DDT was not a secret in 1958. DDT and such chemicals were one of the many outgrowths of the scientific advances of World War II, and the chemical-industrial complex wielded immense power. But, as the official U.S. Fish and Wildlife Service website says, "Carson had long been aware of the dangers of chemical pesticides and also the controversy within the agricultural community. She had long hoped someone else would publish an exposé on DDT but eventually realized that only she had the background as well as the economic freedom to do it."

Have you ever decided to do something because you realized that no one else would do it? Or was capable of doing it? Is this ego or truth? In Rachel's case, probably both.

To write *Silent Spring*, Rachel had to educate herself deeply about the dangers of indiscriminate or casual use of pesticides and other chemical methods of eradicating unwanted insects, weeds, and other organisms. She became an expert on the "side effects" or "unintended consequences" of this kind of use. Ultimately, she found unacceptable what was then an accepted fact: These substances could bring grievous harm to humans as well as death to birds that were no longer there to sing in the spring.

Rachel did not live to observe most of the results of *Silent Spring*, because she died in 1964. Most important, DDT was banned in this country in 1972 and worldwide in 2001 (except for specific uses against mosquitoes). The use of many other pesticides was drastically curtailed and/or better controlled.

One of the most obvious institutional results in the United States was the establishment of the Environmental Protection Agency. That government department has been challenged almost since its inception in 1970. But political wrangling aside, Rachel Carson's work has assured that these concerns will remain paramount and permanent, worldwide: the environment, ecology, and climate, as well as the total interconnectedness of human, plant, and animal life.

Early in this chapter, I told you that many new personal challenges assailed Rachel Carson as the decade of the 1950s began. Let's turn to those now, and think about how she decided to handle them.

She may have been a clear-eyed scientist, but she was also a human being who endured loss after loss. Mary Scott Skinker, the professor who had steered Rachel toward the study of biology in the late 1920s at college and who had become a close friend, had died in 1948. Other friends and colleagues were dying. The people whom she had long supported—her beloved mother, her troubled sister, and a troubled niece—were all dead by the end of the 1950s. The reality of loss was deep and ever-present.

A bright light, even though it was also a challenge, could have been her "motherhood." She was, essentially, the only adult left to parent her late niece's little son Roger Christie and try to guide him through mourning to happiness. (Roger was five years old at his mother's death, and Rachel herself would die only seven years later.)

Spending summers with young Roger Christie on her cherished Southport Island property in Maine inspired Rachel toward a modest book that deserves to be better known. *The Sense of Wonder* first appeared in 1956 as an essay called "Help Your Child to Wonder" in the magazine *Woman's Home Companion.*

The essay was published, posthumously, as a book in 1965 and again in 1998. Like everything Rachel wrote, it is exquisitely beautiful. Here Rachel talks about Roger, to whom the book is dedicated:

> Now, with Roger a little past his fourth birthday, we are continuing that sharing of adventures in the world of nature that we began in his babyhood, and I think the results are good. The sharing includes nature in storm as well as calm, by night as well as day, and is based on having fun together rather than on teaching.

I cannot help but think of Maria Carson and how she helped Rachel to wonder on the farm back in Pennsylvania.

Along with the loss of so many people, the decade of the 1950s also brought questions about the loss of Rachel's health to the forefront—her own private forefront, because few people beyond those closest to her ever knew the extent of her chief illness. Even she didn't know for quite some time. As was common then, the malignancy of the breast tumor that was removed in 1950 (a cyst had been removed from the same breast in 1948) was kept secret from her. And when Rachel learned the truth after subsequent malignancies and surgeries that would mark the rest of her life, she made ongoing decisions aimed at maintaining her privacy—and her ability to function at a high professional level.

It wasn't just the demands of *Silent Spring* that she faced. She was keeping a high-profile and peripatetic schedule. She was rearing an active young child. She was juggling a career as a sought-after public speaker and a prolific writer of pamphlets, bulletins, and articles in all sorts of publications, from the technical to the mass-market.

I know of so many colleagues, friends, and family members who have faced similar decisions in similar circumstances. I expect that you do, too.

As painful as Rachel's decisions were, they seemed to have

been successful. Even shortly before her death in 1964 (one month shy of her fifty-seventh birthday), when the cancer had metastasized widely in her body and she could barely stand upright at a podium to deliver a speech, people thought she was using a cane only because of her arthritis. In fact, news that she had died was shocking.

During her life, not surprisingly, Rachel had frequently experienced health issues that were stress-related, some of them debilitating, for varying periods of time. But breast cancer and the mode of treatment used to treat her—radiation after surgery—was a many-years-long savage experience without respite.

Irony of ironies was that, during the height of her battle, Rachel was working on the "cancer chapters" in *Silent Spring*. She addressed cancer and its links (or not) to the naturally occurring environment:

> The battle of living things against cancer began so long ago that its origin is lost in time. But it must have begun in a natural environment, in which whatever life inhabited the earth was subjected, for good or ill, to influences that had their origin in sun and storm and the ancient nature of the earth. Some of the elements of this environment created hazards to which life had to adjust or perish. The ultraviolet radiation in sunlight could cause malignancy. So could radiation from certain rocks, or arsenic washed out of soil or socks to contaminate food or water supplies.

Chilling are her words about the effects of man-made chemicals and radiation, including:

> The parallels between chemicals and radiation is exact and inescapable . . . if especially susceptible the cell may be killed outright, or, finally, after the passage of time measured in years, it may become malignant . . .

Another vitally important aspect of Rachel's life began in the early 1950s—a new and deep relationship with a place and a person.

Of the many naturally beautiful places where Rachel Carson was "at home" during her life, coastal Maine was possibly the most meaningful. In 1953, she and her mother moved into the cottage they had built on Southport Island. They would be summer residents there (returning chiefly to their home in Maryland) until Maria's death in 1958 and Rachel's in 1964. Rachel's grand-nephew Roger continues to visit the cottage every summer with his family.

On Southport Island in 1952, Rachel had met Dorothy and Stanley Freeman, other summer residents who were admirers of her writing. Admiration turned to friendship, and Rachel and Dorothy became very close. They shared almost all of their joys and reversals with each other.

During their dozen years of friendship that ended with Rachel's death, they corresponded feverishly when they were not together in Maine or visiting each other's vacation home. Dorothy's granddaughter Martha Freeman has collected and edited hundreds of these letters into *Always, Rachel,* a fascinating volume that helps fill out our appreciation of Rachel Carson as a person.

It was no mystery, publicly and in industry and scientific circles and in Congress, that Rachel was researching and writing about DDT and other pesticides. Anticipation was enhanced by *Silent Spring*'s partial serialization in *The New Yorker* (a record-breaking third time a Rachel Carson book had been highlighted in that way) and other high visibility publicity events.

The book was attacked with a vengeance even before it was printed. Its theme, its science, its conclusions—all were criticized. Nor was the author spared. Besides the to-be-expected denunciation of her methods and credentials, her personal life was vilified. A former U.S. government official pointed out that Rachel, as an unmarried woman, was therefore probably a Communist.

Among the readers attracted to *The New Yorker* serialization was President Kennedy. His enthusiastic embrace of *Silent Spring* before its publication led, in the summer of 1963, to Carson's testimony before the Senate Committee on Commerce. Here began the process that would transform her life's work into meaningful public policy. The path to the ban of DDT and to more judicious use of all pesticides, even to environmentalism in all its forms, was paved.

Environmental momentum surged throughout the 1960s. April 22, 1970, saw the first "Earth Day," an event that has been marked annually ever since. President Richard Nixon said that "the 1970s absolutely must be the years when America pays its debt to the past by reclaiming the purity of its air, its waters, and our living environment." Not just America, as country after country began to pay attention and take action. The momentum has changed, but has never stopped.

> President Nixon established the EPA in 1970 to "(pull) together into one agency a variety of research, monitoring, standard-setting and enforcement activities now scattered through several departments and agencies ... (aimed at) effective and coordinated action."

Of all its contributions to the world, perhaps the most important of *Silent Spring*, is the core question that Rachel Carson poses, the question that heads this chapter. To paraphrase the question, Who's to blame? To paraphrase Rachel's response, We all are. I have added my own emphasis to her own words.

The decision is that of the authoritarian temporarily entrusted with power; he has made it *during a moment of inattention by millions* to whom beauty and the ordered world of nature still have a meaning that is deep and imperative.

We can take many lessons on how to make decisions from Rachel Carson's life and work:

1. Pay attention to those in a position to give you good advice. When you are young and your decisions are relatively simple, start with the people who know you best—parents and teachers. As you get older and your decisions become more complex, expand that circle.

2. Educate yourself as deeply as you can. Good decisions are rooted in knowledge and reality.

3. Find your "passion," a combination of your deepest interests and your best abilities. Focus your key decisions here; nothing else is as important.

4. Face no-choice decisions (those you have to make around illnesses or family responsibilities) honestly and squarely, not half-heartedly. Decide to face what you have to face.

5. Be open to serendipity and be willing to make new, different decisions even though they may carry you away from your set path. Decide to set new goals.

6. Recognize that some may attack you. Do not just take it. Stand your ground, but do not get to a low level in your response. Find an elegant way to push back.

PART FOUR
Breaking Boundaries

14

HANNIBAL, JULIUS CAESAR, JOHN KENNEDY

The die is cast.
—JULIUS CAESAR

HANNIBAL IN 218 B.C., Julius Caesar in 49 B.C. and John F. Kennedy in 1961 all made decisions to cross boundaries that were thought to be insurmountable, because of the combination of physical, political, and psychological challenges they presented.

I have never faced such obviously momentous decisions as crossing the Alps or the Rubicon, or breaching the safety of the Earth's atmosphere to go to the Moon. But there have been plenty of decisions, in my personal and business life—as in yours—that have been vital. And I doubt that I am done with making big decisions. I'm sure you are in the same position as I am.

What can Hannibal, Caesar, and JFK tell us?

For Hannibal and Caesar, the goal was Rome and all it represented—Hannibal to vanquish it and Caesar to claim the pinnacle of its power. If a mountain range or a river stood in the way, too bad.

For President Kennedy, the stated goal was rekindling the spirit of America with a project all could relate to—in this case the Moon and what it represented in terms of human dreams. Another implied goal was American victory over the Soviets in the two intertwined battles of the post-World War II Cold War—the Space Race and the Arms Race.

The obvious lesson for you and me—we need to know what motivates us, and therefore what is the purpose of our decisions. Otherwise, there is no true direction, and it's easy to get pulled off course.

The lives of both Hannibal and Caesar were fully shaped by "Rome," that behemoth of the ancient world whose influence spanned close to twelve centuries.

Hannibal was a Carthaginian, born in 247 B.C., when Carthage still dominated the western Mediterranean. It was a fearless sea-faring nation whose prosperity depended on trade, exploration, and acquisition (by any means). However, it was under constant threat by a vicious rival, agrarian-based Rome, whose growth depended on land-based exploration and acquisition (also by any means).

With Carthage dominating the ocean with its navy and Rome the land with its army, little stood in the way of these ferocious and rapacious powers but themselves. Among the many examples of bloody warfare, the three Punic Wars raged from 264 to 146 B.C.

Hannibal's father, Hamilcar, was probably Carthage's most celebrated warrior. He vowed that his three sons would follow in his footsteps: "My boys are lion cubs reared for Rome's destruction." And given what is known of Hannibal's character, destruction of much else as well.

After his father died in battle, or was assassinated, in 229 or 228 B.C., Hannibal swore a vengeance that made his inbred hatred of Rome even more potent. His purpose was clear. He would achieve what his father could not. He would conquer Rome.

In fact, he didn't. Carthage became subsumed into what eventually became the Roman Empire. I'll come back to Hannibal's story and the decision he made that continues to hold the world's imagination, but first I will introduce Julius Caesar.

★   ★   ★

Unlike Hannibal, Caesar was a child of Rome. Its outskirts, at least, as he had been born in 100 B.C. into a poor but "patrician" family living in a downtrodden sector. After his father's death when Caesar was about sixteen, he fashioned a life and career devoted to the accumulation of personal, military, and political power. With title after title and role after role—ranging from high priest (at age sixteen!) to consul to general to permanent dictator—he became quite at home in the Forum, the seat of Roman government.

Highly gifted in many ways, but absolutely ruthless, Caesar used every tool at his disposal—intelligence, cunning, betrayal, execution, military conquest, violence, intrigue, leadership, oratory. His entire life was in the service of Rome's legendary expansion as far west as Spain, across Gaul to Britain in the north, south into Africa and east into Israel.

The decision of Caesar's that lives on in the English language as an idiom for "no turning back" centered on a shallow and insubstantial river that meandered through the countryside about 200 miles from the center of Rome. The Rubicon River marked the northeastern boundary of the portion of Italy that was under Roman control. Coming south from his latest successful military campaign in Gaul—and of necessity, transiting the Alps, perhaps not so much of an ordeal as it was for Hannibal!—Caesar would, of course, pause here.

A new and strict law governed the river. Simply put, a general was required to temporarily put aside his "imperium" (his military command) in order to cross it. This law was aimed squarely at Caesar. Breaching it would be a capital offense—treason—and yet another civil war would result. The men of his army would also be considered traitors.

Caesar knew all this as he stood on the banks of the Rubicon in 49 B.C. and pondered his next step. What had led him to this literal and figurative brink?

I think that the years of doing what came naturally to Caesar—dominating, defeating and surviving—in the service of "the state" blurred his boundaries, in modern terms. The difference between the personal and the political no longer existed. What Caesar wanted was what Rome should want. A law should stand in his way?

After much thought and planning, Caesar decided to push forward. As he did so, according to contemporary historian Suetonius, Caesar uttered, "The die is cast." He and his army crossed the Rubicon and marched on Rome.

Caesar was murdered five years later, in the heart of Roman power, the Forum, by close associates. His betrayal transcended history and has become immortalized in literature. Following the lead of Suetonius the historian, Shakespeare had Caesar utter "Et tu, Brute?" as his "friend" Brutus wielded the fatal knife. As near as he was to his goal of consolidating his power, Caesar was ultimately the victim of the same kind of violent intrigue that was his own specialty.

The denouement of Caesar's story was eerily similar to Hannibal's. The Carthaginian came close, but he never arrived in triumph in Rome. After his astonishing tactical success in crossing the Alps, Hannibal's exhausted army faced the Romans in battle after battle as his men grasped and crawled their way south on the Italian peninsula. But the Punic Wars had more than one front. Hannibal had to withdraw from Italy to assist his brother Hasdrubal in defending Carthage itself from the octopus-like Roman army. Ultimately, Carthage was defeated. Hannibal died far from Rome in 283 or 281 B.C. by swallowing poison to avoid being captured and executed.

But do not consider Hannibal a failure. In pursuit of his goal, he had done the unthinkable. His imagination was as strong as his military prowess. With the Romans dominating the seas surrounding the Italian peninsula—essentially, they were beating the Carthaginians at their own game—the seemingly impenetrable Alps were an effective natural defense. Hannibal turned the tables on the Romans by launching a land-based attack. He brought thousands of men, horses and war elephants up and over the Alps. In the winter, no less. No one had ever done what Hannibal had. His tenacity even inspired the Latin saying "Hannibal ad portas" that persists to this day as an expression of anxiety—"Hannibal's at the gates."

When Hannibal and Caesar made and carried out their decisions, they were not acting as isolated individuals. They needed all sorts of help from all sorts of people. Yes, they were military and political leaders at the pinnacles of persuasion and command. Yes, they had armies that were required to follow their orders.

Was that enough? Think of people whom you respect as leaders. Do they demand your slavish adherence? Or do they strive to inspire your confidence? How do you handle the leadership roles in your life?

Hannibal and Caesar possessed monumental abilities to lead. I imagine that those men must have glowed with personal charisma, because it could not have been easy to follow them. In my years of working with corporate and individual clients, I have never met any successful leaders who were not charismatic. These people were not necessarily popular, though it is easy to confuse popularity with charisma. Popularity ebbs and flows depending on the vagaries of the moment. Charisma is innate and therefore permanent, so it can be possessed but not acquired. And it is a character trait that is more and more vital as high-level decision-making in today's world becomes more and more fraught.

What were the lasting results of Hannibal's and Caesar's decisions? Specifically, I find it hard to say. It is not too much of a stretch to suggest that their decisions be viewed as a densely patterned tapestry whose threads cannot be teased apart. Their decisions are viable today because they shaped the Roman Republic of Hannibal's time and the Roman Empire of Caesar's time into the foundation of Western Civilization.

Some 2,000 years later, John F. Kennedy stood on that same foundation with his decisions about how the United

States would advance global civilization. One decision concerns us here—to commit the United States to the exploration of space and specifically to land an astronaut—the late Neil Armstrong—on the Moon. (Safely, I might add; with a trip back home, too.)

In 1961, when Kennedy became President, Hannibal and Caesar would have recognized the age-old issues of dominance and conquest that were at play. The main players were the United States and the Soviet Union. The two countries, after their World War II alliance against common enemies, had become Cold War adversaries.

But now there was a new frontier—"outer space." Based on work that had begun separately before and during World War II and whose urgency had ramped up during the 1950s, the two nations were building their own space-exploration programs.

Humans have for eons longed to rise up from the earth and thence to break through its life-supporting atmosphere.

Indeed, the "space race" may have begun with da Vinci's fifteenth century "flying machine" or the Wright Brothers' first airplane flight in 1903. And with the end of World War II on all fronts, the U.S. and the USSR turned their massive energies (including many war-related technology advances) in the direction of all that would be needed for success in space. This sort of work is happening again today, as nations and private companies seek economic advantages in troubled times.

The Soviets successfully launched two earth-orbiting satellites in 1957. The accomplishment was astonishing—the first time in all of history that the earth's atmosphere had been pierced. Neither Sputnik I nor II was manned (though the second one held a passenger, Laika the dog, who did not survive the journey) but the effects of this literal breakthrough cannot be underestimated.

Although I was young at the time, I could feel, and see as I looked to my parents, the deep anxiety produced by the knowledge that "they" had beaten "us." What were "they" doing up there, anyway? If a satellite could carry a dog, could it carry a bomb? The threat seemed overwhelming.

Because another race was simultaneously underway—the arms race, based on the two countries' accumulation of nuclear and other "weapons of mass destruction." It was another result of World War II and Harry Truman's decision not many years earlier. As Kennedy said on the day he took the Presidential Oath of Office, "The world is very different now. For man holds in his mortal hands the power to abolish . . . all forms of human life."

Between 1957 and 1961, space-based events came at breakneck speed. And even though the American effort seemed to be holding its own, there was no denying the fact that the Soviets had been "up there" first.

If our two countries had been working as one on space exploration, can you imagine the sense of accomplishment that might have permeated the world?

Instead, when he was sworn in as President on January 20, 1961, Kennedy faced an American public severely demoralized by the Soviets' early victory in the space race and what that might mean for the arms race.

Kennedy addressed the deep national malaise in his inaugural speech:

> To those nations who would make themselves our adversary, we offer not a pledge but a request: that both sides begin anew the quest for peace, before the dark powers of destruction unleashed by science engulf all humanity in planned or accidental self-destruction.
>
> We dare not tempt them with weakness. For only when our arms are sufficient beyond doubt can we be certain beyond doubt that they will never be employed.
>
> But neither can two great and powerful groups of

nations take comfort from our present course—both
sides overburdened by the cost of modern weapons, both
rightly alarmed by the steady spread of the deadly atom,
yet both racing to alter that uncertain balance of terror
that stays the hand of mankind's final war.

His speech's series of "Let both sides . . ." prescriptions contained two that addressed the twin fronts of the Cold War:

Let both sides, for the first time, formulate serious
and precise proposals for the inspection and control of
arms—and bring the absolute power to destroy other
nations under the absolute control of all nations.
Let both sides seek to invoke the wonders of science
instead of its terrors. Together let us explore the stars,
conquer the deserts, eradicate disease, tap the ocean
depths and encourage the arts and commerce.

Kennedy made the national commitment to the Space Race
and to the Moon explicit. He immediately tasked Vice President Lyndon Johnson with assessing where the United States
could dominate the Soviets most decisively.

With Johnson's assessment in hand—simplistically, that the
Soviets could probably orbit the Moon first, but that the U.S.
could actually land a man on the Moon first—Kennedy crossed
his own Rubicon.

Let's again go to Kennedy's own words to examine his Space
Race decision, and the commitment he wanted and needed
from the nation.

In May 1961, he addressed a joint session of Congress to,
basically, ask for the money:

I therefore ask the Congress, above and beyond the
increases I have earlier requested for space activities,
to provide the funds which are needed to meet the
following national goals:

First, I believe that this nation should commit itself to achieving the goal, before this decade is out, of landing a man on the Moon and returning him safely to the Earth. No single space project in this period will be more impressive to mankind, or more important for the long-range exploration of space; and none will be so difficult or expensive to accomplish.

Kennedy got the money.

In September 1962, before scientists at Rice University in Houston (the city that housed the new Manned Spacecraft Center), Kennedy gave what has become known as the "Moon Speech." Its conclusion:

Many years ago, the great British explorer George Mallory, who was to die on Mount Everest, was asked why did he want to climb it. He said, "Because it is there."

Well, space is there, and we're going to climb it, and the moon and the planets are there, and new hopes for knowledge and peace are there. And, therefore, as we set sail we ask God's blessing on the most hazardous and dangerous and greatest adventure on which man has ever embarked.

"Fly-y-y me to the Moon and let me play among the stars. . . ," may have been nothing more than far-fetched lyrics when Bart Howard wrote them in 1954. But they captured a romantic spirit that Kennedy was able to harness in the service of something much more pragmatic—American victory in the Space Race.

Note that Kennedy's Space Race commitment did not assuage America's existential anxiety (indeed and unfortunately, it is now an accepted part of life). As well as you and I remember Sputnik, remember the twin to-the-brink Arms Race events that played out during Kennedy's term in Soviet-aligned Cuba—the Bay of Pigs invasion in April 1961 and Missile Crisis of October 1962.

We all know that Kennedy did not live to see the U.S. achieve his stated Space Race goal—reaching the Moon by the end of the decade. But on July 20, 1969, there was Neil Armstrong, declaring victory by hoisting the American flag on the Moon.

And though the Space Race ended that day, space exploration continued apace, including joint U.S. and Soviet/Russian missions. The Cold War itself ended in 1991, with the dissolution of the USSR, but the Arms Race is alive, now with many more players.

Let me circle back to a phrase in Kennedy's Moon Speech—"we ask God's blessing"—to delve into a delicate but essential area. What is the place of the Divine in the decisions made in the public arena? Privately, of course, we all have our innermost guides, and I know I do not make one major decision without prayer. But what do the stories of Hannibal, Caesar, and Kennedy tell us about civic decisions?

Both Hannibal and Caesar lived in a time of multiple deities from multiple traditions. Gods and goddesses were active and visible in all aspects of life. By the time Kennedy came along, of course, monotheism ruled in America and, publicly, "God" was no secret.

The god Melqart, who hailed from Phoenicia, was associated with the sea and its exploration, and it is said that Hannibal's father Hamilcar dedicated his son to Melqart. It is also said that Hannibal went to Melqart's temple before he set off for Italy and there received a strengthening vision.

In the case of Caesar at the Rubicon, the historian Suetonius related that a man of "extraordinary height and beauty," presumably a divine messenger, led the way across the river, causing Caesar to cry, "Take we the course which the signs of the gods and the false dealing of our foes point out. The die is cast."

In 1954, the Cold War had prompted the addition of the phrase "under God" to the American pledge of allegiance, though this national dedication was nothing new. Our Declaration of Independence cites "God . . . the Creator . . . Divine Providence," while the First Amendment to the Constitution enshrines religious freedom. Published in 1910, our informal national anthem, "America the Beautiful," proclaimed "God shed His grace on thee." As a senator, Kennedy would have begun every session of Congress listening to a prayer from the chaplain. Prayer breakfasts were already normal political fundraising events. The paper currency in Kennedy's wallet bore the words "In God we trust."

Even so, in 1961, it was not yet routine for presidents to close speeches, announcements and other public utterances with the phrase "God bless America." So was Kennedy's "we ask God's blessing" remarkable? In the face of such a monumental undertaking as pledging the nation to go to the moon, I think it was quite natural.

As the first Catholic president, Kennedy endured suspicions that he would be influenced by the Vatican rather than by the Constitution. The Vatican, of course, is a city-state. Was Kennedy quietly reminding us that his strength in decision-making came from no political entity, but from a divine source? Was "we ask God's blessing" an act of quiet bravery?

I don't know Hannibal, Caesar, or Kennedy well enough to speculate on their innermost motivations. I only know what history—and my own imagination—tells me, that core principles must have been present. Do you think that such principles support your own decisions?

Here are the top lessons I take from the decision-making processes of Hannibal, Caesar, and JFK:

1. None of these men could have achieved their goals alone. Most of us need men and women to support us in our pursuits and decisions. Make sure you understand what they want because if you do not, you should not expect their help.

2. In other words, recognize that whatever your goal is, it will be more powerful to the people around you if it speaks to their self-interest. However, that may mean balancing your agenda with theirs. Are you willing to do that?

3. Know your own motivations. Are they really yours or do they come from outside you, whether your family or your culture?

4. Keep your eye on the goal as well as on all the steps needed to achieve it. The forest is made up of many trees.

5. As you take the steps toward your goal, be prepared for both success and the occasional failure. And recognize that what happens at each step may slightly alter what comes next—in other words, be flexible.

6. Know your limitations. If carrying out your decision involves motivating other people to help you, do you have what it takes? Are you a leader? Do you have charisma?

7. Don't operate in a vacuum. Seek information, because even the most mundane piece may be vital. If you are crossing the Alps, what is the weather report?

8. Know your assets. Do you have the people, infrastructure, and money to carry out your decision?

15

ABRAHAM LINCOLN

> Give me six hours to chop down a tree and I will
> spend the first four sharpening the axe.
> —ABRAHAM LINCOLN

THOSE WORDS ARE WIDELY ATTRIBUTED to Abraham Lincoln, without any evidence that he ever uttered them. But they sure sound like something he would have said!

How about these words? "I am a slow walker, but I never walk back." "Be sure you put your feet in the right place, then stand firm." Nope, apocryphal as well.

Here are words that Lincoln really did say: "A man watches his pear-tree day after day, impatient for the ripening of the fruit. Let him attempt to force the process and he may spoil both fruit and tree. But let him patiently wait, and the ripe pear at length falls into his lap."

These are among the many quotations, both real and imagined, that I could easily produce for you to show how Lincoln made decisions. Such quotations speak of a man determined, careful, patient, and dedicated. Maybe even wily and dogged. Just a few of the personal characteristics of our sixteenth and greatest President, who became known as the Great Emancipator because, as all schoolchildren know, "Lincoln freed the slaves."

The man with the pear-tree is one of Lincoln's utterances about the key decision of his presidency. The pear-tree analogy gives us his own picture of himself as he nurtured, and then brought to fruition, the wartime executive order known as the Emancipation Proclamation that, temporarily, freed the slaves or at least began the process. Actual new law would be necessary. What the Proclamation did do, definitively, was to change the course of the Civil War and of American and therefore world history. Its repercussions are felt even today.

Lincoln's presidency was defined by the Civil War. Lincoln was inaugurated on March 4, 1861, and the war began on April 12. The war ended on April 9, 1865, and Lincoln was assassinated on April 15. The centerpiece of both the presidency and the war was the Emancipation Proclamation, published in preliminary form on September 22, 1862, and made effective on January 1, 1863.

> Because of a slight error in its printing, the Proclamation was not ready for Lincoln to sign until late in the day on January 1. In the meantime, he took part in the traditional New Year's Day reception at the White House. When he finally picked up the pen to sign, his right hand was shaking from the exertion of shaking hands with many visitors. He hesitated and massaged his hand until it was soothed. Then he proceeded. He did not want anyone in future years seeing a shaky Presidential signature and thinking that he had had second thoughts.
>
> Self-awareness, another key attribute of Lincoln's character and his decision-making ability.

Why was, and is, the Emancipation Proclamation so important? To answer that question, we must first ask, Why was the Civil War fought?

Why would Americans turn upon each other so thoroughly that 620,000 of them—of us—would die? That horrible number is almost equal to all of our casualties in all the other wars our country has waged.

Consider 117,000 Americans dead in World War I; 418,500 in World War II; 58,000 in Vietnam, and thousands more in Korea, the Middle East, and other locations. This does not even count the wounded, nor all the casualties suffered by the "other side" of our foreign wars. The terrible numbers add up.

Was the Civil War primarily a struggle to define "states' rights" within a federal system ("the Union")? Or was it about "emancipation," the end of the slavery?

Keep in mind that America was not even a century old when the Civil War began in 1861. Our national identity was still being forged. New states were being admitted to the original thirteen, and new territories were being organized into states. The vast sweep of America, from one ocean to another across a richly endowed continent, was, to say the least, diverse—in geography, climate, natural resources and—increasingly—in population and people's goals for themselves. And all states, territories, and people were bound to conform to a framework— our foundational documents, the Declaration of Independence of 1776 and the United States Constitution of 1789.

The Declaration held forth the premises of equality and freedom as aspirations, not yet reality. And the Constitution was not perfect. Almost immediately, ten amendments had to be added and by the time of the Civil War, another two, in 1797 and 1804. (There are twenty-seven today.) The Bill of Rights (those first ten amendments) did not extend rights to anyone beyond white men. And the prosperity of a large swath of the developing country depended on a certain kind of social structure that, while immoral, was pretty much acceptable throughout the entire world—slave labor.

Lincoln knew that the Emancipation Proclamation would bring clarity to the Civil War. Yes, the young country's system of a central Federal government needed to be preserved. But there was a higher principle—slavery in the United States had to come to an end. Slave trading had been banned in the U.S. since 1808, but not slavery itself. The Missouri Compromise of 1820 did put some restrictions on slavery, and the abolition movement was stirring. But laws such as the Fugitive Slave Act of 1850, the Kansas-Nebraska Act of 1854, and others, seemed to strengthen the institution.

Lincoln's overarching goal—the demise of slavery, not just its remission—was achieved in spite of his death. The Thirteenth Amendment to the Constitution was passed by Congress on January 31, 1865, during the final paroxysms of the War. It was ratified by the states on December 6, 1865, eight months after the assassination. The Fourteenth Amendment (granting citizenship to all native-born Americans, including emancipated slaves) followed in 1868 and, in 1870, the Fifteenth Amendment (granting voting rights to all races; the gender of those voting was not addressed until the Nineteenth Amendment in 1920).

None of these rights-granting amendments came easily. The former Confederate states, for example, had to be threatened with losing their rights to Congressional representation if they did not ratify the Fourteenth Amendment. It took until the Voting Rights Act of 1965 to redress many (but not all, as we see today) of the abuses that began almost immediately after the passage of the Fifteenth Amendment. At least a century of struggle was needed to accomplish the Nineteenth Amendment. The Equal Rights Amendment, banning discrimination based on gender, remains in abeyance. It was passed by the Senate in 1972, yet never achieved the necessary ratification by the states.

Young America was not so young when it came to the history of slavery within its borders, nor was it alone in its countenance of human bondage to achieve economic aims. Indeed, the "problem," if I may use such a mundane word for such notorious evil, is as old as humanity. Serfdom, involuntary servitude, forced labor—all these synonyms come to mind.

The money-making possibilities presented by the European "discovery" of the "new world" were irresistible. As early as 1650, captive Africans were forced to work the fertile plantations of the new British, French, and Portuguese colonies. Merchant ships captained by "slavers" grotesquely plied the Atlantic Ocean's "middle passage" of a tripartite economic system that brought (1) European goods to Africa, (2) captured Africans over to the colonies and (3) sugar, tobacco, and other products back to Europe. American slavery was concentrated in those colonies that eventually became the Southern states and, in 1861, those states formed themselves into the Confederacy to challenge the Union in the Civil War.

Abraham Lincoln was not the first world leader to grapple with the horrifying and immoral institution of slavery. One of his predecessors in the effort was William Wilberforce (1759–1833), the British legislator and reformer who dedicated his career and his life to the eradication of first the British slave trade (1807) and then slavery itself in Great Britain (1834). The U.S. slave trade-banning action in 1808 was modeled on Wilberforce's work.

The economic and cultural factors that Wilberforce battled were immense. After all, money was to be made! And people didn't much seem to care about the conditions that produced the sugar for their delicacies and the tobacco for their cigars and all the other material benefits of world trade. But with his spirituality of good vs. evil as his guiding light—and his substantial political and persuasive skills—Wilberforce persisted. He knew that nothing less than permanent change, the kind enshrined in law, was necessary.

Lincoln would have known of Wilberforce's political work, and did have a deep personal repugnance about slavery. Politically speaking, though, he seemed reticent. In 1849, during his only term in the U.S. House of Representatives, he had sponsored a bill that forbade slavery in the District of Columbia. When his two years were up, he went back to Illinois to resume his career as a popular and successful lawyer, but he did not again seek office in Illinois (he had served four terms in the statehouse).

The 1854 passage of the Kansas-Nebraska Act seemed to propel him back into public life. The Act had been sponsored by Illinois Senator Stephen Douglas and, at an event that presaged the famous Lincoln-Douglas debates of the 1860 Presidential campaign, both men gave major speeches in Peoria on October 16 that year. Each speech was three hours long, and I will not try to condense any of the complex arguments. But Lincoln described not only the existence and spread of slavery, but its growing but seemingly casual or inevitable acceptance, saying:

> This declared indifference, but as I must think, covert
> real zeal for the spread of slavery, I cannot but hate.
> I hate it because of the monstrous injustice of slavery
> itself . . . My first impulse would be to free all the slaves.

As Ecclesiastes tells us, there is a right time for everything. I know that timing, good or bad, applies to decision-making. So we should take note of the concept of timing as regards both Lincoln's developing public stance on slavery and the advent of the Proclamation.

Lincoln had in fact written the document many months before its initial publication in September 1862. But he kept it in his desk drawer, so to speak. The War had not been going well for the Army of the Potomac, with the Confederate Army dealing a succession of gruesomely bloody blows in battle after battle. Close advisors urged the President not to act from a position of weakness, while in defeat. Rather, it was better to wait and take advantage of a Union victory.

That victory came, sort of, in the terrible Battle of Antietam (Sharpsburg, to Southerners) on September 17, 1862. This single bloodiest battle of the war (23,000 dead, wounded, and missing on both sides, in the course of one day) had ended in an apparent rout. What was left of the Confederate Army retreated to the banks of Maryland's Antietam River. And there it was allowed to stay overnight. The Army of the Potomac did not press its advantage fully and the delay allowed the Confederates to cross the river to relative safety the next morning.

It was immediately obvious that the Union side had lost the chance to deliver a resounding, perhaps even fatal, blow to the Confederate side. But it did deliver enough of a blow, and "victory" was declared. Certainly, the tide of the war changed, and Lincoln recognized the event that he had been waiting for. Five days after Antietam, he unveiled the Proclamation.

Thus we see that timing is everything, as people other than the writer of Ecclesiastes have said (maybe even Lincoln, who was a master of political timing). Here is another important factor for all of us to consider. Make decisions at the right time! Make them when they can do the most good, and you will advance your goals. Coupled with that advice is the need to be alert and aware of changing circumstances. And to be prepared to act; the best decision in the world may be useless if you cannot carry it out.

Let's take a look at several more aspects of Lincoln's decision-making process in general and as he applied it to the Emancipation Proclamation.

In the four months between Lincoln's November election as President and his March inauguration (the Twentieth Amendment of 1933 moved the inauguration date to January 20), state after state seceded from the Union. In another month, the Confederates made their first attack on Union territory. The crisis had seemed more and more inevitable, and now here it was in reality.

Just as you would have many detailed questions as you approach serious decisions, Lincoln would have pondered these as he began to take actions as a wartime President:

- Was his commitment to ending slavery a useful political posture or his own deeply held moral belief?
- How would he square his personal anti-slavery commitment with his oath to "protect and defend the Constitution," which essentially forbade states' secession yet held slavery to be legal?
- Was a precursor (the Proclamation) necessary before the abolition of slavery could be fully addressed in an amendment?
- What political and public-opinion obstacles would he face?
- How would he identify them and work with and around them?

To answer these and other questions, Lincoln thought ahead, beyond the immediate. To offer a useful cliché, he played chess, not checkers. He seemed to have had the patience to wait until a complete picture began to emerge or conditions were ripe. For example, the Proclamation was not a law; rather, one might say it was an expedient and temporary solution. It was a temporary Executive Order designed for wartime conditions. Its provisions would expire at the end of the conflict.

Lincoln's two-step process (the Proclamation followed by the Thirteenth Amendment very soon after the war's end) reminds me of Wilberforce's focus on abolishing, first, the enabling method (slave trade) and then the evil itself (slavery). In Lincoln's case, there was a gap of months between steps; in Wilberforce's, almost thirty years. Are you, too, prepared to "play the long game," if necessary?

A man of true humility and prudence, Lincoln often turned to others. He sought guidance that would inform, but not dictate, his pursuit of the correct course of action. He habitually gathered opinions and insights from those around him, partly out of simple human curiosity, I'll bet. But this also helped people feel that they were participants in larger decisions that took them into account and that made sense. Instead of being surprises arriving from left field, such decisions were somehow inevitable. Remember the pear-tree analogy Lincoln employed to introduce the Emancipation Proclamation to the public? At that same event, he said, "I have done what no man could have helped doing, standing in my place."

When a decision was made, however, he did not hide behind others. Foreshadowing leaders such as Harry Truman and Margaret Thatcher in the next century, Lincoln took full responsibility. As he told his Cabinet, "There is no way in which I can have any other man put where I am. I am here. I must do the best I can, and bear the responsibility of taking the course which I feel I ought to take."

Lincoln was known throughout his life as an extremely gifted writer and speaker (as was Wilberforce). Astonishing when you remember that he had very little formal education (Wilberforce was well-educated). But in addition to immense intelligence, Lincoln had an innate sense of what to say and how to say it both beautifully and effectively. And he worked at it!

I think that eloquence is part of strong decision-making. Writing and speaking well depend on clarity. You must know your thoughts and your facts and be aware of the needs and expectations of your audiences. You need to have a thesis statement, a clear-cut goal for what you are writing or saying. Just as with decision-making. You need to marshal all the factors that will, or might, affect what you are contemplating.

Beyond his carefully crafted speeches and letters, Lincoln used story-telling (or yarn-spinning) to marvelous effect. He could be ribald, humorous, or wickedly funny, homespun, serious—whatever it took to disarm his audience while he made a point or performed what research professionals have come to call "soft soundings." You can do the same.

Confidence is an overlooked factor in effective decision-making. I don't mean cockiness. I mean the personal strength that is rooted in knowledge, experience, and purpose. Reading biographies of Lincoln and Wilberforce convinces me that they were very strong people. Had they been weak, they never would have overcome personal difficulties (bad eyesight and life-long illness for Wilberforce and less-than-modest beginnings for Lincoln) or withstood the forces of their times.

Not only was he an excellent writer, Lincoln was prolific and seems to have inspired others to be the same. Over 20,000 of his own letters, speeches, and other documents have been archived. At 15,000, Lincoln is said to be tied with Martin Luther for the record of having more books written about him than about any person in history other than Jesus Christ.

Lincoln may have "freed the slaves," but America continues to be haunted by the Civil War and what some have called our "original sin" of slavery.

Vicious disagreements about statues of Confederate generals, for example, are place-holders for larger issues of identity, history, racism, and inequity. Think about lynchings, beatings, murders, and assassinations, about lunch counters and city buses, about violence in minority communities, voter suppression, restricted real estate listings, affirmative action, integration, the 2008 Presidential election—and so much more.

Civil rights activism remains its own war. And theologically, the nature of original sin is that it is forgiven and removed but its effects remain.

Does this gloomy assessment mean that Lincoln's decision about the Emancipation Proclamation was wrong or ineffectual? This is something that all of us worry about as we make decisions large and small.

My answer is a resounding No. Abraham Lincoln's decision was of the highest moral order. It was right, in the true sense of that word. It was good. The changes it caused in America have become worldwide.

I'll close by suggesting a visit to the Lincoln Memorial in Washington DC. If you've been there before, you'll know why. If this would be your first visit, you have much to look forward to. Picture yourself standing there, dwarfed and humble, as you gaze up at the magnificent and massive statue of a brooding, seated Lincoln. What is he pondering? Surrounded by the shadowing, sheltering, and towering classical columns of the Memorial edifice, resolve to make your own decisions—right ones and good ones. They will change your world.

This greatest of American presidents offers us these lessons:

1. Be patient in all you do.
2. Always seek clarity in your actions.
3. Do not accept immorality. Work to change the culture.
4. Work to understand when the right time to act might be. And gather supporters, especially if you are making a controversial decision.
5. Always be humble.
6. When possible use stories and illustrations to make your point.
7. Timing is everything.

16

MUHAMMAD ALI

> My conscience won't let me go . . . just take
> me to jail.
> —MUHAMMAD ALI

THOSE WORDS FROM OVER FORTY YEARS AGO would be today's sound-bite for one of the decisions that boxer Muhammad Ali made that changed the world—his refusal to serve in the Vietnam War when he was drafted in 1967. Especially for African Americans and also for Muslims, he instantly became a symbol for resistance to that war, the scars of which our nation carries even now, almost forty-five years since its end.

Muhammad Ali, at age twenty-five, was already world-famous. He was a symbol to African Americans and Muslims for his world-changing decision in 1964 to discard his "slave name" of Cassius Clay as part of his embrace of Islam. He was a symbol of athleticism, having won Olympic gold in 1960 and the world heavyweight title in 1964. (That was the first time; he would claim it two more times.) Having called himself "the greatest" since he was a mischievous child and a cocksure teenager, he was well on the way to symbolizing the full meaning of "The Greatest." He would become an icon for much more than his athletic prowess.

On the one hand, Ali was a very simple man. He had once been classified 1-Y (not quite 4-F but close enough) by the Selective Service because of his, shall we say, alleged intellectual limitations. He made his living beating up other men; that's the sport of boxing, and he was very good at it. On the other hand, he was quite complex. He reveled—oh, how he enjoyed himself!—in presenting himself as a mesmerizing mass of contradictions who, during his lifetime, attracted and re-pelled many people, sometimes simultaneously.

When he died in June 2016, Muhammad Ali was almost universally hailed. His admirers had never stopped admiring him. Negative attitudes toward him had begun to soften as he dedicated himself to humanitarian work during the long retirement that most professional athletes have. And of course, the public could see him slowly and inexorably disappear into Parkinson's disease, which he endured for thirty-two years.

His condition was heartbreakingly evident in 1996 as he lit the Olympic flame to open the Atlanta games. He struggled to hold the heavy torch, and his body shook violently, but he persevered. The athlete who had handed him the torch in the final step of the long relay process said, "It was all about cour-age. It was written all around his body that he was not going to let (it) do him in. He was still the greatest."

The lead paragraph of his Legacy.com death notice supplied to the public read simply: "Muhammad Ali, the heavyweight boxing champion named Sportsman of the Century by Sports Illustrated magazine, died June 3, 2016."

The news began to break during the evening hours. That night, Paul Simon was performing at the Greek Theatre in Berkeley, California. Just before he sang the last verse of the Simon & Garfunkel classic "The Boxer" (the verse that begins, "In the clearing stands a boxer, and a fighter by his trade . . ."), he paused. He announced that Muhammad Ali had died. There were gasps and then applause from the audience as Simon seg-ued into that verse, with the final line: ". . . but the fighter still remains."

The death of this larger-than-life man was universally cov-ered in the media. Here is but a sprinkling of the headlines of news stories and obituaries:

- "Muhammad Ali Dies at 74; Titan of Boxing and the 20th Century" —*The New York Times*
- "Muhammad Ali: The man who changed his sport and his country" —BBC News
- "Muhammad Ali—boxer, athlete, provocateur—dead at 74" —*Sports Illustrated*
- "Muhammad Ali dies at 74: 'The Greatest' comes home" —*Louisville Courier-Journal*; Louisville, Kentucky, was where Ali was born and grew up, and where he is buried.
- "Muhammad Ali dead at 74: tributes to the greatest of all time" —the UK's *Telegraph*
- "To Muslims the world over, Muhammad Ali was '#The Greatest'" —*Los Angeles Times*
- "'The Greatest' Muhammad Ali Dies at 74: The champion 'shook up the world' and wound up fighting—and beating—a system set against him as hard as he fought any contender and became one of the world's most beloved athletes" —*Ebony*

And then there's this example. The Poetry Foundation website picked up on writer/critic Juan Vidal's National Public Radio tribute, "Muhammad Ali: A Poet In and Out of the Ring." Calling Ali "Whitman in white trunks and a robe," Vidal had written: "He was always drawn to words. And part of Ali's genius was mastering the art of making his words serve his purposes, both in and out of the ring—his playful approach to rhyme often made doubters eat his words, and theirs: "'Henry, this is no jive. The fight will end in five.'"

Yes, Muhammad Ali was a poet. Certainly, his own sort of poet, as we know from his taunts and boasts and various proclamations, all with idiosyncratic rhyming schemes and their own rhythms. He was even credited by *Rolling Stone* as one of the inventors of rap.

Not surprisingly, because poetry is best appreciated when heard aloud, not read on the page, this man who was rumored to be dyslexic and couldn't read easily, was a great raconteur. How Ali could express himself! In his 2004 memoir, a very unusual one written with his daughter Hana Yasmeen Ali, this is on full display. I assume that Muhammad dictated and Hana wrote it all down. The resulting *The Soul of a Butterfly* is captivating.

I hope you're beginning to get the idea of the man Muhammad Ali was.

There are myriad ways to look at Muhammad Ali. In this book on decisions, I will focus on Ali's intertwined decisions to change his name and become Muslim, and to refuse military service. I see in Ali a living example of a person's conscience in the process of being formed. This is not always a pretty picture; actually, pretty or not, it's more like a movie, since for most of us it takes a lifetime. But conscience is integral to making good and important decisions, perhaps even decisions that change the world.

Almost nothing is more personal than your name. Yet it is something that other people—your parents, usually—have given to you. As an infant, you respond to it before you even know what "responding" is. It may be the first thing you learn how to spell. You grow up and go through life with it. Like most people, you automatically accept it.

Muhammad Ali was born Cassius Marcellus Clay, Jr. in 1942 in Louisville, Kentucky. In those days, he would have been called a Negro. His father, obviously, was also named Cassius Marcellus Clay. As was another Kentuckian a few generations earlier, a renowned white Civil War-era planter, politician, and diplomat from Kentucky who espoused abolition. The first Cassius Marcellus Clay freed the slaves he inherited from his father and paid them wages to work for him. As was the practice, many of these slaves would have already been "endowed" with their owner's last name.

In 1964, as part of his conversion from Christianity to the

Nation of Islam, it is said that Cassius "changed his name" to Muhammad Ali. Actually, he didn't choose the name as much as he accepted it from Elijah Muhammad, the Nation of Islam leader. Even so, Ali announced that he had shed his "slave name," moving first to Cassius X and then to Muhammad Ali, because: "I didn't choose it and I don't want it. I am Muhammad Ali, a free name—it means beloved of God, and I insist people use it when people speak to me."

At another time, he expanded on his explanation:

> Cassius Clay is a name that white people gave to my slave master. Now that I am free, that I don't belong anymore to anyone, that I'm not a slave anymore, I gave back their white name, and I chose a beautiful African one.

The name change, among other things connected with Ali's conversion, was seen by many people, thoughtful and otherwise, as being purely confrontational. Many in the boxing world refused to use it. Martin Luther King Jr. said, "When Cassius joined the Black Muslims and started calling himself Cassius X, he became a champion of racial segregation, and that is what we are fighting against." (The two men later reconciled, King calling Ali "a friend of the cause" and noting that, "We are victims of the same system of oppression. Although our religious beliefs differ, we are still brothers.")

And then there was the reaction of Cassius Clay the father. It seemed dismissive—"I'm not changing no name. If he wants to do it, fine. But not me." Not only had Cassius Jr. changed his name, but his other son had, too. Rudolph Valentino Clay had also joined the Nation of Islam and was now Rahman Ali. What was going on? An eternal question, to be sure, between every generation, in every culture.

Boxing, the family business? Known as "Rudy" the future Rahman Ali trained with his brother at Joe Martin's gym. The brothers excelled equally at boxing. Rudy did not qualify for the 1960 Olympics, however, where Cassius won his gold medal. Rudy turned pro in 1964 and retired in 1972, after a career of fourteen wins, three losses, and one draw. He joined the Nation of Islam before his brother did. Laila Ali, Muhammad Ali's daughter born in 1977, was undefeated in all twenty-four fights in her eight-year career (1999–2007) in women's boxing.

More important, and more confounding to me even now, is the fact that the Nation of Islam (whose full name was the Black Nation of Islam) believed in in-your-face separatism. Why would Cassius Clay, a man named for a man who was dedicated to emancipation decide to join such a group? Lend it his prominence and his reputation? Was Cassius Clay merely under the sway of charismatic men such as Elijah Muhammad, Malcom X, Louis Farrakhan, Jeremiah Shabazz, and others?

Consider Ali's childhood and his experience returning home to Louisville in 1960 from the Olympic games in Rome. He had been the darling of the entire U.S. team. He had represented his country well. He won the gold medal for boxing. And yet when he wanted a drink of water out in public, there were two fountains to choose from—his was labeled "Colored" and it was not only forbidden, but dangerous, to use the one labelled "White." The decision was rooted in the racism Cassius experienced and thought deeply about.

You see, Cassius Jr. the boy grew up in a setting still subject to "Jim Crow laws." Abolition Lincoln may have "freed the slaves" with the Emancipation Proclamation in 1863. The Thirteenth, Fourteenth, Fifteenth, and Nineteenth Amendments may have been added to the Constitution to address certain rights (but not yet full voting rights; that came in 1965). But even so long after the Civil War, Kentucky remained a Confederate state at heart. Abolition and emancipation had not yet truly arrived. Not to this day.

From History.com: "Jim Crow laws were a collection of state and local statutes that legalized racial segregation. Named after an insulting song lyric regarding African Americans, the laws—which existed for about 100 years, from the post–Civil War era until 1968—were meant to return Southern states to an antebellum class structure by marginalizing black Americans. Black communities and individuals that attempted to defy Jim Crow laws often met with violence and death."

In Cassius's daily life, segregation ruled. Separate entrances to public buildings, separate seating in movie theatres, separate public drinking fountains, separate schools, separate everything. And "separate" did not mean "equal"—so much that Cassius saw and experienced outside of his home told him that. And beyond; he lived in Kentucky not Mississippi, but he certainly knew what had happened to Emmett Till, a boy not much older than Cassius, in that deep-South state.

Emmett Till was a fourteen-year-old black boy from Chicago who was visiting relatives in Money, Mississippi, in 1955 when he was accused of "insulting" a white woman. The specifics were always unclear. But they were enough for the woman's husband and another family member to track Emmett down, beat him, mutilate him, shoot him in the head, and throw his body into the Tallahatchie River. At his funeral, the boy lay in an open casket for all to see the brutal condition of his body. Emmett's lynching and the trial of his two murderers, who were acquitted, became a rallying point for the civil rights movement. Almost 50 years later, the woman admitted that her husband had forced her to testify, falsely, about Emmett.

Why would Cassius Clay decide to join a group that sought to deepen the separation between the black and the white races? That espoused violence to do so? He may have been a championship fighter, but outside the ring he was known for his gentleness, a quality he never lost.

The answers to all these questions about conversion and name change may really reside in one place. They were Cassius Clay's personal response, as his conscience developed, to the growing unrest unleashed in the early '60s in this country by the civil rights movement. The search for rights of all kinds had always co-existed. Women's rights, voting rights, rights for "minorities" and so on are inseparable. But now the search for African American civil rights was growing larger and stronger. It was becoming a powerful cause and would soon be a full-throated demand. "Black Power" was a magnetic theme. That, I think, is what the Nation of Islam offered to Cassius-soon-to-be-Muhammad, who never minced words:

I am America. I am the part you won't recognize. But get used to me—black, confident, cocky; my name, not yours; my religion, not yours; my goals, my own. Get used to me.

Years later, in his memoir, Ali said simply: "When I became a Muslim, I was on my way to entering what I called 'The Real Fight Ring,' the one where freedom and justice for Black people in America took place."

* * *

When Cassius Clay became Muhammad Ali at age twenty-two in 1964, it took a long time for the public to heed his request to "use it," to call him by what was now his name. Doing so was too uncomfortable. Even many sportswriters, whose bread and butter was covering the continuing exploits of this marvelous athlete, refused. They would not accept his identity. Jimmy Cannon was one who famously had no use for the boxer, saying: "I pity Clay and abhor what he represents." But most came around to the opinion later expressed by William Rhoden of *The New York Times*:

> Ali's actions changed my standard of what constituted an athlete's greatness. Possessing a killer jump shot or the ability to stop on a dime was no longer enough. What were you doing for the liberation of your people? What were you doing to help your country live up to the covenant of its founding principles?

I am not going to treat the virulent controversies that seemed to characterize much of the Nation of Islam in Muhammad Ali's time; they are easily researched and not germane to my focus on Ali's personal decisions.

The year that leader Elijah Muhammad died, 1975, is when Ali decided to fully embrace the ancient Islam faith. (Today, with about 25 percent of the world's population as practitioners, Islam is the second largest religion in the world.) Ali's experiences and his conscience had brought him to that decision. Again, he was initially derided. But for the rest of his life, Ali adhered visibly to the faith. Not always perfectly, he admitted, but who of us is perfect anyway? As Pope Francis said in another context, "Who am I to judge?"

As his boxing career continued and then ended and he moved more fully into the roles of humanitarian, peace advocate, and philanthropist that had begun to attract him, Ali also became an icon of the Muslim world. The coverage in the *Los*

Angeles Times at the time of his death included an article replete with analysis and praise from both "everyday" Muslims and Muslim scholars and leaders. I've selected only two statements out of so many:

> He promoted Islam in a noble way. He showed tolerance, the aspiration for peace, understanding and social justice. He showed that faith in God puts a lot of strength into the body.

> He was not an ordinary boxer. I'm proud of him as a Muslim who fought against terrorism and extremism, and who has always been a model of a great Muslim.

And now to the second decision of Muhammad Ali's that rocked the world, starting in 1966 and playing out until 1971, to resist the military draft. Refusing to be inducted into the Armed Forces, refusing to fight in Vietnam ("I ain't got no quarrel with them Vietcong"), even refusing alternative service—but accepting his punishment—all these actions sprang fully from his adherence to the Nation of Islam, of which he called himself a religious minister.

As required of all eighteen-year old "male citizens" of the United States, Cassius Clay registered with the Selective Service in 1960. He was initially given the top classification of A-1 (hey, he was an Olympic athlete!). That designation was later downgraded to 1-Y ("unqualified to serve" except in a national emergency) when testing disclosed his severe dyslexia. (Ali joked, "I only said I was the greatest, not the smartest.")

March 8, 1965 is the "official" start date of the U.S. involvement in the Vietnam War, which had been fomenting since 1955. As we all know, our limited involvement grew rapidly, and Vietnam had become a national emergency. Hundreds of thousands of American soldiers were on the ground, and young men were being drafted at the rate of tens of thousands per month. With so many troops needed, maybe not everyone had to be 1-A. Test-score parameters were lowered, and all of a sudden Ali's were within range and he was re-classified upward. Not only was he now eligible to be drafted, he *was* drafted.

In early 1966, he got the summons. He immediately requested deferment on religious grounds. More than a year's worth of legal back-and-forth delay ensued. But Ali's life as a "conscientious objector (CO)," which some called "draft dodger," had begun. Though opposition to the war had begun to grow, public support still seemed firm. Ali was widely excoriated for his stance.

During this time between being summoned and actually being drafted, Ali continued to box and win, box and win, title after title. Many found it ironic that a CO could fight as viciously as he did. With the perspective that time gives, I wonder if he was fighting for his life, for he knew it would soon change. Did he think about all the other young men, soldiers who were, literally, fighting for their lives, and ours as fellow citizens? There are no easy answers to any of this.

The home page of the Selective Service System, a U.S. government entity, sets out its mission: "To register men and maintain a system that, when authorized by the President and Congress, rapidly provides personnel in a fair and equitable manner while managing an alternative service program for conscientious objectors." Registration is required by law, but the "draft" does not exist as an ongoing process, but is implemented during certain times of war (not all) and then expires. Here's how the website exhorts eighteen-year-old men to register: "It's What a Man's Got to Do. It's quick, it's easy, it's the Law." Currently, the registration rate is over 90 percent.

Muhammad Ali did not invent draft resistance, or war resistance, for that matter. Both have histories as long as humankind. In every American war, there have been men (women have never been drafted in this country) who would do everything from refuse to register, to refuse to be inducted, to agree to be inducted but not take up arms, to leave the country. And for every American war, there have been men and women who, nonviolently or not, have exercised their right to object.

In April 1967, Ali finally arrived at the induction center, but that's all he did. He would not answer any questions because he was being called "Cassius Clay." Once the authorities relented on that matter, Ali sought status as a conscientious objector. He was offered the alternative of being inducted as a noncombatant. That meant that agreeing to serve as something other than a soldier—to fight in exhibition matches, perhaps, as entertainment for the troops. That he also refused, knowing that he would be indicted and tried for his decision.

In June, he was found guilty and given the maximum punishment, five years in prison and a $10,000 fine. He also had to surrender his passport. Legal appeals (all the way to the Supreme Court) kept him out of prison. But he soon found himself in another kind of prison—he could no longer box. He was disqualified by state boxing commissions throughout the country. Without a passport, he could not travel to boxing venues outside the country.

As a black man and as a Muslim, Ali was accustomed to slurs. But now he was being shamed as a "draft dodger." And along the lines of the adage "sticks and stones may break my bones but names will never hurt me," Ali found out what really hurt. Not being able to pursue the only profession he was actually qualified for, he paid a real price for his stance.

During Ali's "exile," he remained very visible. Among other things, be began making speeches on college campuses, where he found friendly audiences. We all know what 1968 brought in this country—the King and RFK assassinations, violent demonstrations on campuses, at political conventions, and at other sites, deaths of student demonstrators at the hand of the government, the presidency turning over from Lyndon John-

son to Richard Nixon. The tide of public opinion was changing in so many ways. In so any ways, the American culture was
changing as well. And Ali managed to thrive.

In 1971, the saga of Muhammad Ali's draft resistance was
over. The Supreme Court ruled that, indeed, his claim for CO
status was legitimate and his prosecution for refusing induction
was wrong. He was free of the restrictions against boxing and
could resume his career.

Yet he had lost four years in his prime as a boxer. There is
much speculation on how much greater "The Greatest" would
have been if his career had not been stalled in the way it was.
Even so, between 1971 and his retirement ten years later, there
were thirty more fights and only six losses. In his entire career,
he fought sixty-one times, taking an estimated 200,000 hits.
Imagine that.

I had the privilege of attending several of Muhammad Ali's
fights, and will never forget those spectacles, both inside and
outside the ring. Each man would seem beyond human in his
size and strength, even to a big man like me (6'4" tall, an inch
taller than Ali was). Ali's style and athleticism would be on full
display—fast and flashy feet that let him dance around his opponent, his fists low, the only boxer who could get away with
that unusual stance, ready to strike faster than lightning. (He
was always innovating his sport. Later in his career, when he
was older and slower, he employed a unique "rope-a-dope"
strategy that seemed to allow him to rest while he tired out his
opponent.)

And the scene outside the ring—clouds of cigar smoke,
clamoring voices cheering and hooting, glamorous and fash-
ionably dressed men and women, blinding flashbulbs from all
the cameras. But there was never such an attraction as Muhammad Ali.

And the scenes inside the locker rooms after the bouts! Ali
almost always on a high of victory, spouting poetry off the top

of his head, celebrating himself and his greatness, loving every minute of being "on stage."

In the heady early years of Ali's career, the atmosphere of professional boxing was well-reported in the media, and the coverage of Ali as an individual athlete was intense. This continued after his "comeback" in 1971, even if boxing itself didn't occupy the same place in modern culture as it once had.

Always, there were the legions of professional newspaper, magazine, TV and radio sportswriters and columnists, all the names that avid fans would know and follow. There were all the professional photographers. There were widely known "men of letters" such as George Plimpton and Noman Mailer with their unique ways of plying the writing trade. (Mailer's *The Fight,* which chronicled the "Rumble in the Jungle," the Ali-Foreman 1974 battle in Zaire, is a classic beyond the world of sports coverage.) And there were fellow celebrities such as Frank Sinatra (who photographed the 1971 Ali-Frazier fight for *Life* magazine—and made the cover!) and Jackie Gleason (who wrote a column for the *New York Post* the morning of the 1964 Ali-Liston championship match, inaccurately predicting Ali's defeat). Because Ali was happy to be a celebrity, there were countless others, in the world of media and beyond, who found him a ready, willing, and able subject.

When even Muhammad Ali had to admit that his career as a boxer was over in 1981, he moved into a new stage of life. There was rediscovery of his family. There were public appearances to make that didn't involve getting beaten up. The days of name-changing and draft-dodging were far in the past. There was much philanthropic and humanitarian work to be done around the world, including visiting and comforting sick children wherever they were. There was the Dalai Lama to meet. There was his developing love for the Special Olympics. And there was the inevitable decline from the combined effects of age and disease.

The statement released by President Barack Obama the day after Ali's death cited the fulcrum-point of the famous name-change decision as evidence of "a spiritual journey that would lead him to his Muslim faith, exile him at the peak of his power, and set the stage for his return to greatness with a name as familiar to the downtrodden in the slums of Southeast Asia and the villages of Africa as it was to cheering crowds in Madison Square Garden."

Calling Ali "a man who fought for what was right," and referring to the draft-refusal decision without saying those words, Obama continued, "His fight outside the ring would cost him his title and his public standing. It would earn him enemies on the left and the right, make him reviled, and nearly send him to jail. But Ali stood his ground. And his victory helped us get used to the America we recognize today."

Noting that, "He wasn't perfect, of course," Obama concluded, "Muhammad Ali shook up the world. And the world is better for it."

Before I close, I want to answer a question that maybe you didn't even have—Why and how did Cassius Clay decide to become a boxer in the first place? Many writers have their versions of this story that took place in 1954, when the new red bicycle that young Cassius had gotten for Christmas was stolen. I'll use Muhammad Ali's words from his memoir:

> I was so upset I went looking for the police to report it. Someone directed me down to the gym run by a policeman named Joe Martin, who was teaching young boys to box in his spare time. I told Mr. Martin I was gonna whup whoever stole my bike. I was half-crying and probably didn't look too convincing. I remember Mr. Martin telling me, "Well, you better learn how to fight before you start challenging people that you're gonna whup." I joined Mr. Martin's gym and began boxing with a vengeance.

Joe Martin, a white man who ran the only integrated gym in Louisville and was a local civil rights leader, introduced Cassius to "a Black man name Fred Stoner, who taught me how to jab." Martin coached Cassius all the way to Olympic gold in 1960. Immediately after that victory, the young boxer turned pro and that part of the men's relationship ended. They remained friends until Martin's death in 1996.

It's "easy" to write about decisions long ago, made by people who are long gone. The decisions I write about here happened not really so long ago—in the 1960s. Muhammad Ali's life and decisions have certainly been well-examined over the years. I can't quantify how many (hundreds?) of books and (millions?) of words have been written about Muhammad Ali, or how many times he was photographed or interviewed (thousands?). Given that Ali died only in 2016, there is undoubtedly much assessment that still lies ahead. Even so, I am confident that what he can teach us about decision-making can stand the test of time. Consider:

- What is the connection between freedom and decision-making? Recall that Ali said, in connection with changing his name: ". . . I am Muhammad Ali, a free name . . . now that I am free . . ." If you are under any constraints at all, can you actually make a decision? And would your decision necessarily be a "bad" one? Is freedom, whether psychologically or physically, a prerequisite to any kind of decision-making?
- Be prepared to take full responsibility for your decisions and their outcomes. Ali did not hide behind anyone, no matter how vindictive public reactions were to his decisions.
- Be prepared for criticism.
- Sift carefully through all the elements involved. Ali's decisions were, perhaps, more complex than those

that most of us face. But even the simplest present more than one side to consider.

- Give constant attention to developing your conscience, your core values, your principles. These are what will give you true guidance.

17

MARTIN LUTHER

> My conscience is captive to the Word of God . . . it
> is neither safe nor right to go against conscience. I
> cannot do otherwise.
> —MARTIN LUTHER

THIS IS A HARD CHAPTER for me to write because I am a practicing Roman Catholic, and I am certain to receive criticism from
some leaders in my Church. But I have become an admirer of
Martin Luther because of the way his conscience led him to
change the way individuals think about religion. In doing so,
he spurred the Protestant Reformation that changed the entire
institution of Christianity.

Indeed, like Muhammad Ali almost five centuries later, as
you read in the previous chapter, Luther would follow his conscience as the guiding principle of his decision-making process
and indeed his life.

"Conscience" is perhaps too spiritual a concept to be found
in today's public discourse, and it is easy to wonder if it is anyone's guiding principle anymore. Commonly defined as "an inner feeling or voice viewed as acting as a guide to the rightness
or wrongness of one's behavior," conscience is very personal. It
is something we all have, but it isn't issued to us ready-to-use,
as part of a "conscience tool kit." It is the work of a lifetime to
develop and hone conscience so that it is a reliable guide. Like
Martin Luther, Muhammad Ali, and so many others, I rely on
my conscience.

I believe conscience (however we name it) is the foundation
of good decision-making. Without a North Star, a compass,

guiding lights, core values, or strong foundations, it is very hard to know that our actions are the right ones. Instead, they may be right only by accident or chance. And it is difficult to know what the effects of decisions, right ones or not, will be. We are all familiar with unintended consequences.

Luther constantly tested his own conscience by measuring it against God, who was the center of his life, and serving God's will. We see this not merely from the externalities of his life (he was an Augustinian monk and priest) but from his actions.

Specifically, his posting of the "Ninety-Five Theses" in late 1517 rocked and permanently redefined the Christian and therefore the Western world. The Theses were firmly rooted in Luther's conscience. They were the prime mover of the Protestant Reformation.

In framing the central decision of Luther's life, I will of necessity gloss over a great deal of a very complicated subject. In some ways, what more can I add? According to the Christianity Today website: "It has been said that in most [religious] libraries, books by and about Martin Luther occupy more shelves than those concerned with any other figure except Jesus of Nazareth. Though difficult to verify, one can understand why it is likely to be true."

Biographers and historians aside, the man himself wrote an almost uncountable number of books, catechisms, sermons, brochures, treatises, letters, and hymns. His translation of the Bible into German, coupled with the then-recent invention in Germany of the printing press (see Chapter 7 about Johann Gutenberg) made the Word of God accessible to "common" men and women in a way that is still groundbreaking. His Ninety-Five Theses are his seminal document.

What did the Ninety-Five Theses actually say? I will not recount all of them here, as the modern era enables you to find them easily via your computer's search engine. They all focus on the scandal-ridden practice of "indulgences" for the remission of sin. Here are just three of them:

No. 27—"They preach only human doctrines who say that as soon as the money clinks into the money chest, the soul flies out of purgatory."

No. 36—"Any truly repentant Christian has a right to full remission of penalty and guilt, even without indulgence letters."

No. 39—"It is very difficult, even for the most learned theologians, at one and the same time to commend to the people the bounty of indulgences and the need of true contrition."

Luther's lifetime of 1483–1546 is nestled right into the middle of the Renaissance, generally defined as the years 1300–1700. The Renaissance was characterized by the spirit of inquiry—explorations and discoveries of all kinds, inventions, new answers. Because many "old ways" were being discarded, as much as those four centuries brought openness, they also brought insecurity and instability. And worse, as they were indelibly marked by "the Inquisition."

The Inquisition movement was promulgated by the Roman Catholic Church and the Holy Roman Empire, the dominant and commingled entities of Western life. The Church was founded shortly after Jesus' death in the year 33 and thrives globally today. The Empire (think of a form of government called "holy" because it was "dedicated to God," but was not a church or a religion) held sway from 962–1806. Headquartered in Rome and in Germany, respectively, these were spiritual and political powerhouses almost beyond reckoning.

Using extreme measures to enforce all kinds of religious orthodoxy, the Inquisition began early in the century of Luther's birth and extended into the twentieth century in one form or another. The form that was aimed squarely at the Protestant Reformation, known as the Roman Inquisition, was established right around the time of Luther's death.

Ultimately, Luther's life showed him to be a Renaissance man who generally did not fear what was new and untested and unorthodox. He himself was excommunicated and fled imprisonment by the Church. Fearlessness plus a conscience makes a formidable combination. This is another aspect of his decision-making that we can all learn from—facing the unknown with a strong attitude. Not only Luther, but all the other people portrayed in this book brought great strength to their pursuits.

Luther was born in Eisleben in Saxony, Germany, that country being the seat of the Holy Roman Empire. Like pretty much everyone else, he was Catholic, baptized when he was one day old. Religion did not seem to be a defining characteristic until he rather abruptly decided to become a monk in his early twenties. It was the first of many decisions in his life that had unintended consequences.

Martin hid this decision from his family because it would have displeased and surprised them, had they known about it. His father Hans fully expected him to become a lawyer and find a place in the family's mining business. Loyal filial advice would assure continued success for the business, which Hans had begun once he was able to break free from his roots as a peasant. A lawyer's presumed prosperity would mean that mother and father would be well-supported in their old age.

Martin was a dutiful son. He became well-educated so he could achieve his strong-willed father's goal for him. By 1505, he held bachelor's and master's degrees from the University of Erfurt. Studying the law would be next.

Martin excelled academically and his whole life showed how much he enjoyed study, so achieving a law degree should have been easy for him. But he had turned away. He did not want to be a lawyer, and didn't even know what he wanted to be or do instead. The death of a friend and other personal crises affected him deeply. He enrolled in law school in Erfurt but did not attend, delaying the unpleasant parental conversation that he knew lay ahead.

Because we have all been in similar positions, let me pause here and make something clear. Several paragraphs ago, I said that Luther generally had no fear. That was as an adult. At this time in his life, right after university and facing who knows what, I think the young man was beset by all the usual uncertainties and doubts that most of us harbor but few admit. But making a decision based on fear, which is what becoming a monk initially was, inevitably set him up to make his monumental world-changing decision.

Back to my story.

One night, riding on horseback from his home in Eisleben (his father still ignorant of Martin's internal struggle) back to Erfurt, Martin encountered such a ferocious thunderstorm that he thought he would die. He called out to a familiar saint, so we are told, "Help me, St. Anne! I will become a monk!" The storm ceased. His spur-of-the-moment vow had caused his rescue, Martin reasoned, and his rescue was a message from God that he had an obligation to carry out the vow.

Instead of facing his father's wrath, Martin confided to a few friends that he would seek refuge behind the protective doors of the Reformed Congregation of the Eremitical Order of St. Augustine at Erfurt. He did so two weeks after the thunderstorm, in mid-July 1505.

He took his vows as a monk the next year and was ordained a Catholic priest in 1507. His family, invited to witness his first Mass, finally knew why Martin had disappeared. Too late, apparently, for a law career. But not too late for his father to ask him how he was sure the message had not come from the Devil?

This anecdote reveals another key aspect of successful

decision-making—taking responsibility. In Luther's case, he did not want to do what was expected of him but feared the consequences of admitting it. I could almost say that a deus ex machina (or a saint ex machina) had come to his rescue and given him the excuse he needed. May I suggest that young Luther's decision-making path in this case is not to be emulated. Though let's admit, we've all fallen back on handy excuses at decision-time.

Luther entered the monastery in 1505. There he embraced what became his defining mission—to find and follow God in ways that went beyond his childish knowledge.

The time until 1517 (the year of the Ninety-Five Theses) was an often difficult time filled with study, discourse, and prayer, as well as fasting, discipline, and many other challenging practices and pursuits. Sometimes in the isolation of his cloistered monastery, sometimes in the company of his fellow Augustinians and sometimes in crowded classrooms. But he thrived. One of his many unforeseen accomplishments was becoming a popular and admired professor, having been ordered to earn a doctorate by his superiors.

After his youthful period of fear, and for the rest of his life, Luther was drawn to study as well as debate, discussion and the lively exchange of views. Dissent didn't bother him. He seems to have possessed a balance between being introverted and being extroverted. He learned how to seek and take counsel.

Monastic life is not supposed to be easy, and Luther did not find the path to knowing God and doing God's will—to developing a mature conscience—to be easy either. I will focus on one example, his extreme scrupulousness about confessing his sins.

As many Christians do, Martin Luther subscribed to the belief that humans are corrupt and ever sinful. They deserve punishment. Believing this way keeps the focus more on the wrath and vengefulness of God (Old Testament) and less on God's forgiveness and mercy (New Testament). More on Adam and Eve's original sin and expulsion from Eden (Old Testament) and less on the redemption and triumph of Jesus' crucifixion and resurrection (New Testament).

Given his focus on the overwhelming need to appease God, Luther was driven to confess his sins, over and over, for hours and hours, to ever more weary priests. He scoured himself for shreds of evidence of wrongdoing and would re-present the same sins. Unable to accept forgiveness or even do his assigned penance properly, he was caught in an unbreakable cycle.

It was both the patience and a few well-placed words of Luther's long-time confessor, Dr. Johann von Staupitz, that may have finally broken the cycle and shown Luther a more fruitful way.

The confessor grew weary and exclaimed, "Man, God is not angry with you. You are angry with God. Don't you know that God commands you to hope?"

Luther's reaction: "If it had not been for Dr. Staupitz, I should have sunk in hell." I think he began to examine the real reasons for his spiritual anger—the Catholic Church's scandal-ridden practice of indulgences. And the Ninety-Five Theses were his expression of the hope that Dr. Staupitz urged him toward.

Luther agonized that his and everyone else's sins, even those forgiven in confession, would be punished both in this life and the next. And in doing so, he also wrestled with the reality of "indulgences."

This practice of "free passes," as it were, was established by the Church to mitigate punishment for sins. Beginning as a benign way to encourage prayer and good works, indulgences literally came to represent overwhelming greed and scandal in the Church. In simple terms, you could buy your way into heaven. Or someone else's, if they had already died and you feared they were suffering in purgatory. Along the way, you were providing money for Church authorities (up to and including the Pope) to use in their own opaque ways, often involving personal enrichment. Always, true spirituality was subverted.

Luther's spiritual obsession with his own sinfulness collided with his intellectual discomfort and growing anger regarding the institution of indulgences. Something must change!

So, he did what any good scholar would do—he decided to formulate his objections into a series of thesis statements that he would offer up for debate and discussion. Surely this openness (the adage "sunlight is the best disinfectant" comes to mind) would begin the process of rectifying what had become a terrible practice. His hope was that, having "seen the light," the Church would correct itself.

Lore has it that Luther nailed his Theses to the doors of the Wittenberg Castle Church, a dramatic gesture that was a definitive break from Catholicism and signaled the birth of the "Lutheran Church."

This is not true.

Luther wrote his Theses in a letter dated October 31, 1517, that he delivered or sent, or had someone else deliver, to Archbishop Albrecht of Mainz, who was a major player in the world of indulgences. Luther wanted to engage in a colloquy. This is evident throughout the document, starting with the subtitle, "Disputation on the Power of Indulgences." He did not want to break from the Church, just reform it, change it, maybe even just tweak it. In the humble and straightforward words of his preamble, he asked Archbishop Albrecht to

> deign to glance at what is but a grain of dust, and for the sake of your episcopal kindness, listen to my request. Under your most distinguished name, papal indulgences are offered all across the land for the construction of St. Peter . . . [sinners are] convinced that souls escape from purgatory as soon as they have placed a contribution into the chest.

People leaked documents in those days, too. The contents of his letter began to spread far and wide among people we would now call "thought leaders." The broadside version that we imagine Luther nailed to the doors, like a poster, was the work of an entrepreneurial printer making the most of that recent invention, the printing press. A couple of weeks later, this version was indeed affixed in some way to the doors of the Castle Church, which served as a sort of community bulletin board.

The Ninety-Five Theses were officially public, and the battle was joined. The impact of this today is almost without measure.

More than one historian has likened Luther's action to a spark that ignited some very dry kindling. The subsequent wildfire spread beyond his control, and its flying sparks set off new conflagrations far from the source. As one historian wrote, ". . . he had no idea."

It's likely that Luther had some idea of the danger of the fire he had sparked. A century earlier, in July 1415, the Bohemian reformer Jan Hus was executed—for heresies in connection with many of the same issues that Luther grappled with. Execution aside, the other similarities between Hus and Luther are striking—education and priesthood in particular. Hus is considered one of a number of significant precursor figures in the Protestant Reformation.

Luther's action took place at an ideal time, even though the danger of the Inquisition loomed. Almost accidentally, our Renaissance man found a ready audience, people themselves searching for religious and (given the Church/Empire intertwining of institutional power) political change. In other words, Luther's action had unintended consequences. Here we see, twinned with "conscience," Luther's brand of decision-making.

Unintended or not, the results of Luther's decision to "go public" with his Ninety-Five Theses were incontrovertible. According to the Christianity Today website:

> Luther's legacy is immense and cannot be adequately summarized. Every Protestant Reformer—like Calvin, Zwingli, Knox, and Cranmer—and every Protestant stream—Lutheran, Reformed, Anglican, and Anabaptist—were inspired by Luther in one way or another. On a larger canvas, his reform unleashed forces that ended the Middle Ages and ushered in the modern era.

The Ninety-Five Theses were born of a free spirit of inquiry, but they ran squarely into the deadly blockade of the Inquisition. Luther wanted discussion and discourse about indulgences and all the other matters he thought the Church should address and correct—and would correct, he thought, once the "right way" was pointed out. I doubt he wanted what came his way in 1521—to be excommunicated and then to face trial by the Inquisition. The results were that he was thrown out of the Catholic Church, stripped of his priesthood, and found guilty of heresy. However, the Edict of Worms, which meted out other punishments as well, was never fully enforced; eventually it was reversed.

Luther quickly returned to his life's work, because there was much to be done. Indulgences were only one of his many concerns, and his accomplishments were many and far-reaching. When Luther died in 1546, his casket was carried through those famous doors and buried beneath the altar of the Wittenberg Castle Church, where it all began.

The fires Martin Luther sparked with his Theses and all

those unintended consequences could not be extinguished. They burned on steadily. Luther's efforts at reform began to succeed (and turn into "Lutheranism") and the Protestant Reformation became permanent.

In the late twentieth century and into the twenty-first, a series of official "dialogues" began to take place aimed at rapprochement between Catholicism and Lutheranism. Such efforts to "ease conflict" include Anglicanism as well. Unintended consequences?

Before I close this chapter, I want to tell one more story that shows, in very human form, Luther at work as a decision-maker.

The fires of reform that were crackling away as a result of the Ninety-Five Theses soon spread to Catholic convents. Usually cloistered, these were the literal and spiritual homes for vast numbers of consecrated women ("nuns") who had taken their own vows of chastity, poverty, and obedience (similar to Luther's). Following a vocation as a nun was almost a counter-cultural decision in times before and after Luther, when marriage was the expected life path for women. In fact, the convent was a decent option for women who did not want to be forced to marry. However, as yet another (un)intended result of the Luther-inspired reform, many convents were summarily closed, freeing—or dumping—the nuns back into the community. Many other nuns made their own choice to leave their convents. In either event, what were these women to do?

Luther decided to take direct responsibility for a dozen nuns who had taken refuge in Wittenberg. He managed to find husbands for eleven of them, but Katharina (Katie or Katy) von Bora, was languishing unclaimed. To the surprise of everyone, including himself and Katie, he almost impetuously announced that he would marry her. She, impetuously or not, agreed.

Luther was forty-two and Katie twenty-six at the time of their marriage. History tells us that the former priest and the former nun enjoyed a happy, loving, successful, and sustaining life together. They had six children (sadly, two died at young ages) and augmented their family with many foster children who came and went over the years. University students flocked to discourse and debate in the household of Herr Professor Luther. I visualize many scenes of happy chaos. Perhaps Luther had remembered his monastery confessor Dr. Staupitz's admonition about hope and leapt into yet another decision with unintended consequences.

Of the people in this book, Martin Luther seems to present lessons on how not to make a decision, good or otherwise. Enroll in law school when you don't want to be a lawyer, but don't tell your father, who's paying the bills? Instead, sneak off to a monastery and stay there in secret until you've made your final vows, which you then invite your father to witness? I'll grant that these were the actions of a young man, but even as a mature man of forty-two, Luther's days of abrupt action were not over when he "jumped" into marriage. Even the work that changed the trajectory of his life and of Christianity, the Ninety-Five Theses, was introduced without much thought as to the consequences.

But like the good professor that he was, Luther has much to teach about how to make a decision:

> **1.** Strive for a balanced approach. On the one hand, root what you do in logic and facts, and do your research. If your father thinks you should become a lawyer, find out what law school and the career of law are all about. If you do not want to be a lawyer, don't go to law school. At the same time, be open to cultural, creative, and spiritual influences that often seem to defy logic or can't be quantified. Was it truly God who directed Luther to the monastery?
>
> **2.** Educate yourself, as I have advised elsewhere in this book. I've noticed that most people who claim that

they make decisions "from the gut" are also pretty well informed.

3. Think about "consequences" in relation to decision-making. Serendipity seems to apply only to positive outcomes, and while it's nice to experience "happy accidents," you can't count on that happening. How much should you think everything through? Can you game out every single action? Can you say with certainty that if you take that action, this will be the result? But if you take this action, that will be the result? On the one hand, on the other hand? What if other people pick up your decision like a fumbled football and begin to run away from your goalpost toward theirs? What if something stupid, unpleasant, negative, or terrible comes about?

4. If you have a prayer life, as we know Luther did, take it to prayer! This is not a way of evading the decision. Many people find that times of prayer, meditation, reflection, discernment—times when we withdraw a bit from the hurly-burly of life—help clarify the path ahead. Vacations can be fruitful for decision-making, too.

5. Take all the time you need to mull things over. Speed is not always necessary. Certainly, some decisions fall into the "strike while the iron is hot" time-frame— or they are happening in emergency or life-and-death situations. But make sure you are not falling prey to scheduling pressures (your own or someone else's), which are often artificially imposed.

6. If there is an ironclad deadline, be careful of waiting until the last minute to decide what to do. Spend the time between now and the deadline carefully.

7. Don't dither, either. Don't allow small, mundane decisions to take on too much importance. Make them, and move on. Don't let them distract you from the more important larger decisions.

8. Do not let fear force you into a decision that you cannot change and that will shape your life. Step back and take a considered approach.

9. Welcoming input (and knowing how to evaluate it) is characteristic of effective adult decision-making.

10. Have the courage of your convictions. Regardless of whether he nailed the Theses to the church doors or mailed them in, Luther went public with them. He never backed down from his conclusions about the evils of indulgences.

11. Be prepared to be attacked, and be prepared to take responsibility for your decision. One word here will suffice—Inquisition.

12. If you have no game plan, all of the consequences of a decision will be unintended. I think Luther was familiar with that reality. But even though "the best laid schemes o' mice an' men / Gang aft a-gley" (to quote the poet Robert Burns), it is still vital to think through the ramifications of your decisions before you implement them.

13. No matter how much work went into them, some decisions are simply the result of serendipity ("the occurrence and development of events by chance in a happy or beneficial way"). This can lead people to subscribe to the theory that "it's better to be lucky than smart." I say instead, "Chance favors the prepared mind." Do your homework, do the spadework—and serendipity may follow.

18

MALALA YOUSAFZAI

> But there was no decision to make. This was my
> calling. Some powerful force had come to dwell
> inside me, something bigger and stronger than me.
> —MALALA YOUSAFZAI

MALALA YOUSAFZAI, as the world knows, was shot in the head by the Taliban on October 9, 2012, as she rode home on the school bus in the Swat Valley, Pakistan. Malala was fifteen at the time. She survived the attack, recuperated in England, and has continued her education. She was awarded the Nobel Peace Prize in 2014 for her "struggle against the suppression of children and young people and for the right of all children to education."

Can a child, an adolescent, a young person—make a world-changing decision? Is someone ever too young?

Let's take a look at Malala's story, because none of this came out of the blue. The "struggle" the Nobel Committee cited, was a decision that was so deeply embedded into her character that, at age fifteen, it had already become her way of life. And continues to be.

Seemingly from birth, Malala loved education. Her biographical material makes much of the fact that she sought to emulate her father, Ziauddin Yousafzai, who was so dedicated to education that he had founded his own school, the one she attended. Such "private" schools are not uncommon in Pakistan.

But Ziauddin's school and his outspoken daughter became

special targets of the Taliban. The fundamentalist group had issued an edict against educating girls and death threats against the entire family (mother Toor Pekai Yousafzai and two sons). The school was forced to close for a time and had re-opened shortly before Malala was shot.

You might say that the child was merely following the example—or the dictates—of the father (who was supported in all endeavors by the mother). That the child made no decisions on her own. That happens in families all the time. I can think of many examples in my own life—involving my parents and the decisions they made for me when I was young, and about how my wife and I did the same for our sons. None of these decisions involved defying the Taliban and bringing danger to our family. But, that may not be the right way to look at what Ziauddin did. Were his decisions part of doing what parents claim we always try to do—leading by example?

Do you ever think about the phrase "an accident of birth"? It means that none of us are responsible for the circumstances of our birth—who our parents are, our family, our nationality or state or town, our genetic make-up, economic status and so on.

Among the things that Malala was not responsible for: That she was a first-born daughter in a culture that values boys over girls; that she was born into a troubled country being over-run by violent extremists. But it was also an accident of birth that she had two parents who were, by all accounts, as dedicated to her welfare, education, and growth as they were to that of her two younger brothers. It seems to me that Malala took what she was given and decided to run with it.

By the time she was shot in 2012, Malala had shown by her own example that she recognized her "accident of birth." Her dedication to education for girls was in fact her own decision based on parental example. Consider her words, written just a year later in her autobiography:

I was very lucky to be born to a father who respected
my freedom of thought and expression and made me
part of his peace caravan and a mother who not only
encouraged me but my father too in our campaign for
peace and education.

At an even younger age than fifteen, Malala was already an
ardent activist. She blogged for the BBC on the oppressions of
life under the Taliban and was the subject of a *New York Times*
documentary. She made speeches often, including one entitled
"How dare the Taliban take away my right to an education."
The year before she was shot, she won both the International
Children's Peace Prize and Pakistan's first Youth Peace Prize.
As the Taliban's noose ever tightened around her country, her
family, and her safety, Malala's outspokenness and visibility
grew. As she wrote in her autobiography, "I decided I wasn't
going to cower in fear of [the Taliban's] wrath."

In the years since she survived the Taliban assassination attempt, Malala has become a global symbol for the cause of education for girls specifically and for the welfare of all children.
Not even a year after she was shot, she addressed the "Youth
Takeover" at the United Nations. Two years almost to the day
after she was shot, the Nobel Committee announced that she
would share the 2014 Peace Prize with Kailash Satyarthi, who
made his name with international peaceful protests on behalf
of children. Even with constant visibility while traveling the
world to event after event, she completed the studies necessary
to be accepted in 2017 into Oxford University (which fact she
announced on her new Twitter account). Also in 2017, Malala
was designated a United Nations Messenger of Peace "to help
raise awareness of the importance of girls' education."

Malala is still enveloped in the support of her family, which
left Pakistan to settle in the UK. *The Economist,* noting that
"Pakistani education has long been atrocious," included the

following in a detailed and dismal examination of the current status:

> From 2007 to 2015 there were 167 attacks by Islamic terrorists on education institutions . . . When it controlled the Swat River valley in the north of the country, the Pakistani Taliban closed hundreds of girls' schools. When the army retook the area it occupied dozens of them itself.

Malala has written two books. The first, *I Am Malala,* was published a year after her shooting and tells, with the help of writer Christina Lamb, of her early life in Pakistan and the event that put her onto a new trajectory. Published in 2017, the second book is for children, *Malala's Magic Pencil.* In it, young Malala yearns for a special pencil that would let her do all sorts of special, interesting things, including drawing "a lock on my door, so my brothers couldn't bother me." I think every child wants a lock like that. Eventually, she describes what we adults will recognize as an intention, a determination, a decision: "I knew then that if I had a magic pencil, I would use it to draw a better world, a peaceful world."

Time will tell us how Malala's decisions as a girl, a teenager, a young adult, and into the future will all play out, how world-changing they will be. My hope is that the answer is—immensely.

Malala's story offers all of us one overarching lesson about decision-making that will help us all lead better lives:

If you are a parent or other adult in a position to influence children and young people, remember how important your own example is. The decisions you make on behalf of others may turn out to be the template that helps form their lives.

If that's all you glean, that's enough. But there are many other lessons to take:

1. Have courage to do the right thing, whether it is large or small.

2. Understand you may be attacked and plan for that in advance. I mean physically attacked, as well as the more expected verbal criticisms.

3. Recognize you may be a symbol for others and prepare for that in ways they will embrace and admire. And behave that way.

4. Follow your decision. Give it a chance to shape your life.

5. Do not give up.

6. Depend on each other. Know whom you can trust, and be that trustworthy person to others to the best of your ability.

7. Seek education and take every other opportunity to broaden your knowledge of the world and its people.

AFTERWORD
by Klaus Schwab
Founder and Executive Chairman,
World Economic Forum

As you finish reading this book, you may find yourself wondering: How could the lessons from world leaders and historical figures ever apply to my life? How could I put myself in a situation where I can change the course of history, like the people discussed in this book? And if I do ever get to such a make-or-break moment, how do I make sure I make the right choice?

It isn't necessary to put such a heavy burden on your shoulders. I've learned that it is near impossible to predict the exact course of your own life or career, let alone that of the world at large. It is better to approach your life and career one small decision at a time and always with a positive mind-set. This approach will pay off over time. I'll give just a few examples to make the point.

At the beginning of his life, Johann Gutenberg could have never dreamt of becoming Europe's leading publisher. Nor could Picasso have wanted to become the most renowned Cubist painter. Henry Ford could not have wanted to become the biggest automobile manufacturer, or Dag Hammarskjöld the U.N. secretary-general. The things they later became most known for simply didn't exist yet.

Similarly, many young people today dream of becoming the CEO of a large company. You might want to walk in Bob Dilenschneider's footsteps, as he had a distinguished corporate career before becoming an acclaimed author. But he didn't become CEO because he aimed for that title when he was young: back then, the concept "Chief Executive Officer" didn't even exist. It only gained popularity in the 1960s.

Indeed, as you find your way in life, you shouldn't worry about how to put your name in the history books. It is much more important to live your life here and now in a way that is valuable to you and to those around you. Every day we make decisions that can positively change us. To show the "courage of conviction" in those recurring daily moments, as Bob wrote, is what really matters.

Take the case of Malala, whom I had the pleasure to meet. Her aim was not to become the world's most known activist for girls' education. She wanted to defend her right and that of other girls in her village to go to school. It was a goal she was willing to fight for every day, and that made a difference in her life and those around her immediately—whether that would win her a Nobel Prize or not.

Or take the case of Pierre and Marie Curie. They didn't become France's most successful and beloved scientists overnight. They spent many years behind their books and in their labs, before making the discoveries that would turn them into Nobel Prize–winning scientists. To paraphrase the quote from Picasso Bob Dilenschneider offers: Inspiration exists, and breakthroughs can happen, but they have to find you working.

Ultimately, we all find what "makes us tick." For Rachel Carson, it was caring for and sustaining our ecosystem and biodiversity. For Eli Wiesel, it was to preserve the memory of the "Shoah," and make sure it happens "never again." For Louis Pasteur and Alexander Fleming, it was to contribute to a better public health with their discoveries in vaccines and antibiotics.

This "purpose" comes to us somewhere along our lifetime, and we cannot hurry it. But we can make sure that when we find out what it is, we are ready to fulfill it or contribute toward achieving it. To do so, I would agree that two crucial aspects are: educating yourself and making sure you care for and involve your loved ones. These elements constitute the pillars of any successful life.

When you have these elements in place—you found your purpose, you prepared yourself through education, and you surrounded yourself by those you love and trust—you only need to persevere. Indeed, if we stick to our moral compass, and always try and do what is right, we will prevail. Such is the lesson of Muhammad Ali, Mahatma Gandhi, Malala, and many others in this book.

These are all lessons that I learned along the way, as I looked for and found my purpose in life. Growing up during the Second World War and its aftermath, I understood from an early age how important it was for countries, organizations, and people to collaborate. But it wasn't until I studied, traveled, and met my wife, that I was able to build what has become my life's work: The World Economic Forum.

As I look back on fifty years of trying to "improve the state of the world" by bringing together stakeholders from all over and all walks of life, I would add just one more element to Bob Dilenschneider's lessons on decision-making: We must always maintain a positive mind-set. Nothing else nurtures good decisions better than positive energy.

There will always be hurdles along the way. You may make mistakes or face unexpected negative externalities—as we saw with Martin Luther. But if you keep your head high and maintain positive energy, you will always end up in a better place than when you don't. As Bob Dilenschneider wrote: In the face of adversity, "do not lose heart."

If you do that, you remember your roots and the values you learned, and apply them throughout your life, you will be sure to achieve greatness—whether it ends up in history books or not.

Best of luck!

ACKNOWLEDGMENTS

I wrote this book to help make life better for people.

Every day we make hundreds of decisions—some small, some significant—that mark our lives. How people make those decisions is critical to their future.

This book captures vignettes on twenty-three individuals who made decisions that shaped the world and whose stories stretch over time from 218 B.C. to right now.

There were so many that helped with this book, starting with Susan Black, a friend of more than forty years, who wrote draft after draft and who did incredible research; to Joan Avagliano, whom I have worked with for decades, who kept all moving in the right direction and who added value at every turn; to Michaela Hamilton, my editor, a female Maxwell Perkins, who provided insights and direction.

These three provided invaluable insights at every turn.

I owe a great debt to my friends, Steve Forbes—a businessman and thinker and journalist of real caliber; and Professor Klaus Schwab, who started the World Economic Forum and who has included me in WEF events since 1983. Klaus gave me the best advice I have ever received at his club in Geneva about ten years ago. It has shaped my life.

There are many more to acknowledge and thank starting with Vito Racanelli, one of the best journalists I know, for his wisdom and insights; F. Craig Johnson, Pastor of Christ Lutheran Church in Aurora, Oregon, who was instrumental in our research on Martin Luther; Linda J. Lear, arguably the foremost authority on Rachel Carson for her time to discuss why this ecologist is so important and belongs in this book; and the staff at the Canby Public Library in Canby, Oregon.

Thank you to The Dilenschneider Group interns of 2017 for their research and thoughtful suggestions: Daniel Gross, Maximilian Meanwell, James Psathas, Peter Psathas, and Cynthia Sciabica; and to Linda Smith, Margarita Bravo, Kelly Lawrence, and Andrea Fekete who helped bring this project to a close.

Steve Zacharius, Chairman, President, and CEO at Kensington, my publisher, deserves special thanks for all he does for so many.

And, of course, thanks to my wife, Jan, who has read and given encouragement on each of my eighteen books.

No statement of acknowledgement would be complete without mention of my supportive family: Jack, my brother; Mary and Martha, my sisters; my sons, Geoffrey and Peter; and my niece, Ricia Harding.

INDEX

Acceptance of responsibility for
    decisions. *See* Responsibility,
    taking for decisions
Active listening, 21
Advisors, role in decision-making,
    16, 19, 20, 100, 101, 167
Albrecht of Mainz, 198–99
Ali, Hana Yasmeen, 177
Ali, Laila, 179
Ali, Muhammad, 174–90
    background of, 177–78, 179–80
    boxing athleticism of, 186–87
    decision-making lessons of,
        189–90
    decision to become a boxer,
        188–89
    decision to change name, 7,
        177–79, 181, 182
    decision to resist draft, 7, 174,
        183–86
    legacy of, 175–77, 183, 188
Ali, Rahman, 178–79
American Civil War, 164–72
    Lincoln and Emancipation
        Proclamation, 7, 163–66,
        170–71
Antibiotics, 119, 121–22
Arms Race, 157–58
Armstrong, Neil, 156, 160

Assembly line, 103–4, 107
Atlanta Summer Olympics (1996),
    175
Atlas Preservatives, 62, 63
Atomic bombing of Hiroshima and
    Nagasaki, 3, 6, 11, 12, 17–18
Attention, paying, 47, 78, 115, 126,
    148
Auschwitz concentration camp,
    36, 45

Balanced approach, to decision-
    making, 202
Banking, 95–101. *See also*
    Giannini, A. P.
Bank of America, 100
Bank of Italy, 96, 98, 99–100
Barber, David, 113
Basques, 27–28
Battlefield paintings, 30–31. *See
    also* "Guernica"
Battle of Antietam, 169
Bay of Pigs Invasion, 160
Becquerel, Henri, 132, 133–34
Benz, Karl, 103
Bergen-Belsen concentration
    camp, 42, 45
Berger, Joseph, 44
Bombing of Guernica, 28–29

Bootstrapping, 96–97
Brady, Mathew, 30
Brutus, 154
Buchenwald concentration camp,
     37, 41, 42
Buna Werke (Monowitz)
     concentration camp, 36–37
Bunsen burner, 119, 122–23
Bush, George W., 8

Caesar. *See* Julius Caesar
Calvin, John, 76
Cannon, Jimmy, 182
Carson, Maria, 139, 140, 144, 146
Carson, Rachel, 137–48, 212
     background of, 139–40
     decision-making lessons of, 148
     decision to write *Silent Spring*
          and expose DDT, 7, 137–38,
          141–48
     personal challenges of, 139,
          143–45
Carthage, 152, 154–55
Catholic Church (Catholicism),
     75–76
     Gutenberg and, 84, 87–88,
          90–91
     Joan of Arc and, 72, 75–76
     Kennedy and, 161
     Luther and, 75, 191–204
Cave paintings, 30
Centralization, 111
Chain, Ernest, 122
Charles VII of France, 72–74, 75,
     78
"Charnel House, The" (Picasso),
     32
Cheesecake Factory, 112
Chipotle, 112, 113
Christianity. *See also* Catholic
     Church; Religious faith
     in France, 75–76
     Luther and, 191–204
Christie, Roger, 143–44
Churchill, Winston, 17, 18
Church of England, 76

Civil rights, 51, 172–73, 181
Clay, Cassius Marcellus, 177–78
Clay, Cassius Marcellus, Jr. *See* Ali,
     Muhammad
Cold War, 52, 53, 156–61
Columbus Savings and Loan, 96
Congo, 53, 57
Congressional Gold Medal of
     Achievement, 42
Conscience, 7–8, 19, 78, 190,
     191–92
"Conscientious objector (CO)",
     184
Consequences of decision, 106,
     126, 203, 204. *See also*
     Unintended consequences
"Consequences of War" (Rubens),
     30, 31
Constitution of the United States,
     165–66
Conventional wisdom, 126
Copley, John Singleton, 30
Core values, 59, 190
Courage, 19, 70, 77, 204, 208,
     212
Creativity, 32, 35, 70
Credit unions, 97
Criticism, 126, 190, 208
Cuban Missile Crisis, 160
Curie, Eugene, 130
Curie, Eve, 134
Curie, Irene, 134–35
Curie, Marie, xii, 128–36, 212
     background of, 130–32
     bad decision of, 134–35
     decision-making lessons of, 136
     decision to persevere after
          husband's death, 7, 128–30
     Nobel Prize, 128, 133–34
Curie, Paul-Jacques, 130
Curie, Pierre, 128, 131–34, 135,
     212

Dalai Lama, 187
Darwin, Charles, 142
Dawn (Wiesel), 41–42

Day (Wiesel), 41–42
DDT, and Carson, 7, 137–38, 142–48
Deadlines, 203
Death marches (Holocaust), 37–38
Decision-making. *See also specific figures*
    author's fascination with, 5
    enjoying the process, 1–2
    Forbes on, xi–xiii
    role of motive, xii–xiii
    Schwab on, 211–13
Declaration of Independence, 165
De Gaulle, Charles, 76
Diary of Anne Frank, The, 45–47
Dilenschneider, Jan, 39–40, 206
Dilenschneider Group, The, 5
Discernment, 20, 78, 203
Dogged decision-making, 120
Donner Party, 40
Douglas, Stephen, 168
Draft resistance, and Muhammad Ali, 183–86
"Dream and Lie of Franco" (Picasso), 29
Dreams (dreaming), 6, 79, 126

Earth Day, 147
Edge of the Sea, The (Carson), 141
Edict of Worms, 200
Eiffel, Gustav, 76
Einstein, Albert, 40–41
Einstein and the Rabbi (Levy), 40–41
Elizabeth I of England, 60
Emancipation Proclamation, 7, 163–66, 170–71
Emergencies, decision-making during, 29, 124, 136, 203
Employee turnover rate, 102
Employee wages, and Henry Ford, 7, 102, 104–5, 106
Environmental Protection Agency (EPA), 143, 147
Equal Rights Amendment, 166
Equivocation, 25–26, 34

Experts, role in decision-making, 19, 20

Faith. *See* Religious faith
Falklands War, 6, 60–61, 63–68, 69, 70–71
    timeline, 64–65
Fall-back plans, 93
Family, role in decision-making, 20, 21–22, 63, 69–70, 71
Fearlessness, 126, 194, 195–96, 204
Fifteenth Amendment, 166, 180
Fight, The (Mailer), 187
Fish and Wildlife Service, U.S., 138, 140–41, 142
Fleming, Alexander, 7, 119–23, 212
    decision-making lessons of, 125
    decision on antibiotics, 119, 120–22
Flexibility, in decision-making, 59, 89, 162
Florey, Howard, 122
Forbes, Steve, xi–xiii
Ford, Henry, 102–6, 107, 211
    assembly line and, 103–4, 107
    decision-making lessons of, 106
    decision to pay workers living wage ("$5 Day"), 7, 102, 104–5, 106
Ford Motor Company, 102–5, 107
Foreman, George, 187
Forgiveness, 43, 47
Fourteenth Amendment, 166, 180
Franco, Francisco, 24, 29, 33
Frank, Anne, 42, 44–47
Frazier, Joe, 187
Freedom, and decision-making, 38–39, 189
Freeman, Dorothy and Stanley, 146
French Revolution, 76
Frost, Robert, 2
Fugitive Slave Act of 1850, 166

Gandhi, Mahatma, 48–52, 57
    assassination of, 51
    background of, 54–55

Gandhi, Mahatma *(cont.)*
  decision at train station, 49–51
  decision-making lessons of, 59
  decision to pursue world peace,
    6, 52
Germ theory of disease, 120, 123
Giannini, A. P., 95–101
  background of, 96
  decision-making lessons of,
    100–101
  decisions in banking business, 6,
    95–100
Giannini, Luigi, 96
Gilded Age, 99
Gleason, Jackie, 187
Goals, 6, 7, 92, 93–94, 148, 162
Gold Rush, 96, 99
Goya, Francisco, 30
Great Depression, 61, 100, 110,
    140
"Guernica" (Picasso), 31–34
  background on, 23–25, 29–30
  color palette of, 32
  decision to paint, 6, 23, 31–33
  symbols in, 31
"Gut," xi, 203
Gutenberg (Man), 83–84, 91, 94
Gutenberg, Johann, xii–xiii,
    83–94, 211
  background of, 84–85, 86
  decision-making lessons of,
    92–93
  decision on printing press, 6, 83,
    86–92
  money-making attempts of, 83,
    85–86, 88
Gutenberg Bible, 83, 90–91, 92–93

Hammarskjöld, Dag, 48, 52–59,
    211
  assassination of, 52, 53
  background of, 54, 55–56
  decision-making lessons of, 59
  decision to pursue world peace,
    6, 52–53, 56–57, 58–59
  Nobel Peace Prize, 57

  Secretary-General of the UN,
    52, 56–57
Hammarskjöld, Hjalmar, 55–56
Hand-washing, 120, 124–25
Hannibal, 7, 151–52, 154–55
  decision-making lessons of, 162
  decision to cross the Alps, 151,
    154–55, 162
Henry VIII of England, 76
Higher purpose, 35, 71, 78, 94,
    101, 212–13
Hitler, Adolf, 24, 28, 36, 44, 61
Honesty, 126, 138
Howard, Bart, 159
Howard Johnson (HoJo), 107–9,
    110–14
Hugo, Victor, 76
Humphrey, Hubert, 58
Hundred Years' War, 73–74, 75
Hunger strikes, of Gandhi, 52
Hus, Jan, 199

I Am Malala (Yousafzai), 208
Immigration crisis, 44, 47
Immorality, 39, 165, 167, 173
"Indulgences," 197–98
Inner voices
  decision-making and, 77–78
  Joan of Arc's decision to obey, 6,
    72–75, 76–77
Inquisition, 193–94, 200, 204
Institute Curie, 129
Iraq war, 34
Islam, 76
  Muhammad Ali and Nation
    of Islam, 174, 178–79, 181,
    182–83

Jackson, Andrew, 16
Jenner, Edward, 122
Jim Crow laws, 179–81
Joan (Spoto), 77
Joan of Arc, 72–79
  decision-making lessons of, 78–79
  decision to obey divine voices,
    6, 72–75, 76–77

Johns, Jasper, 30
Johns Hopkins University, 139
Johnson, Howard, 107–15
  background of, 109–10
  decision-making lessons of,
    114–15
  decision to pursue franchising, 7,
    107–9, 110–13
Johnson, Lyndon, 158, 186
Julius Caesar, 7, 151–54, 155
  decision-making lessons of, 162
  decision to cross the Rubicon,
    xii, 4, 153–54, 161

Kansas-Nebraska Act of 1854, 166,
  168
Karma, 47, 184
Kennedy, John F., 7, 151–52, 155–61
  Carson and *Silent Spring,* 147
  decision-making lessons of, 162
  decisions on Space Race and
    Moon landing, 158–60, 160
  Hammarskjöld's death, 52, 53–54
Kennedy, Robert F., 185
King, Martin Luther, Jr., 51, 178,
  185
"Kitchen cabinet," 16
Koch, Robert, 122
Korean War, 66
  casualties, 165

Lafayette, Gilbert du Motier,
  Marquis de, 76
Laveran, Charles, 122
Lear, Linda, 137–38, 141
Levy, Naomi, 40–41
Lincoln, Abraham, 163–73
  decision-making lessons of, 173
  decision-making process of,
    169–71
  decision to publish Emancipation
    Proclamation, 7, 163–66,
    170–71
  pear-tree analogy, 163, 171
Lister, Joseph, 122
Lives of the Saints, 72

Loans, 95–96, 98
Luck, 113–14, 206–7
Luther, Hans, 194
Luther, Katharina, 201–2
Luther, Martin, xii, 172, 191–204,
  213
  background of, 194–96
  decision-making lessons of,
    202–4
  decision to defy Catholic
    Church, 7–8, 191–201
  Ninety-Five Theses, 75, 91,
    192–93, 197–201, 202

McArthur, Douglas, 17
McCain, John, 38–39, 40
McCain, John S, Jr. "Jack," 39
McDonald's, 109, 112
McLuhan, Marshall, 83
Madoff, Bernie, 43–44
Mailer, Norman, 187
Mainz University, 90
Malala. *See* Yousafzai, Malala
Malala's Magic Pencil (Yousafzai),
  208
Man, John, 83–84, 91, 94
Marcus, Robert, 40–41
Martin, Fernando Martin, 28–29
Martin, Joe, 188–89
Mauriac, François, 41
Meyer, Danny, 113
Michael, Saint, 73
Micro-lending, 96–97
Military draft, and Muhammad
  Ali, 183–86
Missouri Compromise, 166
Mitterrand, François, 134
Monet, Claude, 76
Montgomery Bus Boycott, 51
Moon landing, 158–60, 160
Moore, Charles, 67, 68
Mussolini, Benito, 24, 28

Napoleon Bonaparte, 76
National Peace Award for Youth,
  207

Nation of Islam, 174, 178–79, 181,
    182–83
Nazi Germany, 33, 36–38, 44–47
New Yorker, 146, 147
New York Times, 17, 42, 44, 51, 60,
    176, 182, 207
Nicholas of Cusa, 87–88
Night (Wiesel), 36–38, 41–42, 45, 46
Nightingale, Florence, 122
Nineteenth Amendment, 166, 180
Nixon, Richard, 147, 186
Nobel, Alfred, 57–58
Nobel Peace Prize
    of Hammarskjöld, 57
    for UNICEF, 134
    of Yousafzai, 205, 207
    of Wiesel, 42
Nobel Prize, 57–58, 133–34
    of Marie and Pierre Curie, 128,
        133–34
No-choice decisions, 148
"No turning back," 153–54

Obama, Barack, 42, 188
O'Neill, Eugene, 114
Operation Rügen, 28–29
Origin of Species (Darwin), 142
"Outside the box" thinking, 7, 70
Oxford University, 3, 62, 207

Pacific Ocean theater of World
    War II, 15–16
Paris International Exposition
    (1937), 24, 25, 29
Parks, Rosa, 51
Partner, role in decision-making,
    20, 21–22, 63, 69–70, 71
Passion, finding, 148
Pasteur, Louis, 7, 76, 119–23, 212
    decision-making lessons of, 125
    decision on vaccination, 119,
        120, 121–22
    germ theory of disease, 120, 123
Pasteur Institute, 123
"Pasteurization," 121
Patience, 7, 173

Patton, George, 17
Penicillin, 120, 122
Pennsylvania College for Women,
    139
Pépin, Jacques, 111, 113
Perspective, on decisions, 6, 47
Pesticide use, and Carson, 7,
    137–38, 142–48
Petticoat (Eaton) affair, 16
Picasso, Pablo, 23–35, 211. *See also*
    "Guernica"
    art periods of, 27
    background of, 26–27
    decision-making lessons of,
        34–35
    decision to paint "Guernica," 6,
        23, 31–33
    use of symbols in art, 31–32
"Pilgrim mirrors," 88
Plimpton, George, 187
Polonium, 133, 134, 135
Powell, Colin, 34
Prado Museum, 26
Prejudices, 21, 50, 70–71, 95
Presidential decision-making, 14, 17
    JFK and Moon landing, 158–60,
        160
    Lincoln and Emancipation
        Proclamation, 7, 163–66,
        170–71
    Truman and atomic bomb, 3, 6,
        11, 12, 17–18
Printing press, 6, 83, 86–92
Problem solving, 104, 106, 115,
    125
Protestant Reformation, 75–76,
    90–91, 191, 201
Punic Wars, 152, 154
Purpose in life, 35, 71, 78, 94, 101,
    212–13

Rachel Carson (Lear), 137–38, 141
Radioactivity, 132–36
Radium, 133, 134
Rauschenberg, Robert, 30
Reagan, Ronald, 42

Reckless decision-making, 120, 121, 125
Religious faith, 13, 71, 78
 Joan of Arc's decision to obey divine voices, 6, 72–75, 76–77
Responsibility, taking for decisions, 71, 189, 195–96, 204
 Ali and, 189
 Hammarskjöld and, 53–54
 Lincoln and, 171
 Luther and, 195–96, 204
 Thatcher and, 68, 71
 Truman and, 11, 16, 21, 68
Rhoden, William, 182
Risk-taking, 126
Roberts, Alfred, 61–62
Rockefeller, Nelson, 34
Roentgen, Wilhelm, 132
Roosevelt, Franklin Delano, 12, 17
Rubens, Peter Paul, 30, 31
Ruiz y Blasco, José, 26–27

Sackville-West, Vita, 77. 79
Saint Joan of Arc (Sackville-West), 77. 79
Salk, Jonas, 122
San Fernando Royal Academy of Fine Arts, 26
San Francisco earthquake of 1906, 97–98
Satyagraha, 51
Satyarthi, Kailash, 207
Saul of Tarsus, 49
Schmidt, Helmut, 63–64
Schwab, Klaus, 211–13
Sea Around Us, The (Carson), 141
Second-guessing decisions, 16, 19
Segregation, 179–81
Selective Service System, 184
Self-confidence, 100, 172
Self-limitations, 162
Self-motives, xii–xiii, 162
Selma to Montgomery marches, 51
Semmelweis, Ignaz, 7, 120, 123–25
 background of, 123–24
 decision-making lessons of, 127

 decisions on hand washing, 120, 124–25
Sense of Wonder, The (Carson), 143–44
September 11 attacks (2001), 40
Serendipity, 148, 203, 204
Shaw, George Bernard, 77
Silent Spring (Carson), 7, 137–38, 141–48
Simon, Paul, 175
Sinatra, Frank, 187
Skinker, Mary Scott, 139, 143
Slavery, 164–71, 172
Soul of a Butterfly, The (Ali), 177, 181, 188–89
South Africa, 50–51, 55
Southport Island, 143, 146
Space Race, 156–61
Spanish Civil War, 23–24, 27–28, 32. See also "Guernica"
Special Olympics, 187
Spoto, Donald, 77
Spouse, role in decision-making, 20, 21–22, 63, 69–70, 71
Sputnik, 156
Stalin, Joseph, 17, 18, 24, 28
Standardization, 103–4, 107, 111
Staupitz, Johann von, 197, 205
Steer, George, 28
Stengel, Casey, 16
Stephenson, Phoebe, 61
Stratton-Porter, Gene, 139
Suetonius, 154, 161
Suez Crisis, 57, 66

Taliban, 205–6
Thatcher, Denis, 60, 62–63, 69
Thatcher, Margaret, 60–71
 background of, 61–63
 decision for Falklands War, 6, 60–61, 63–66
 decision-making lessons of, 70–71
 gender question, 65–66
 governing philosophy of, 63–64
 Truman compared with, 68, 69

Thinking "outside the box," 7, 70
Thirteenth Amendment, 170, 180
Till, Emmett, 180–81
Torture, 39
Transamerica, 100
Treaty of Westphalia, 75
Truman, Elizabeth "Bess," 13, 16, 21, 69
Truman, Harry, 3, 11–22, 157
  acceptance of responsibility for decision, 11, 16, 21
  background of, 12–14
  background to decision, 15–16
  decision-making lessons of, 19–21
  decision to use atomic bomb, 3, 6, 11, 12, 17–18
  governing philosophy of, 14–15
  Thatcher compared with, 68, 69
Try again, 125
Twain, Mark, xiii, 83
Twentieth Amendment, 169

Under the Sea-Wind (Carson), 141
Unintended consequences, 106, 126, 142, 192, 200–201, 203
United Nations Messenger of Peace, 207
University of Erfurt, 21, 194–95
University of Paris, 128–29
University of Stockholm, 56
Uppsala University, 56

Vaccinations, 119, 121–22
Van Hensbergen, Gijs, 25
Vidal, Juan, 176
Vietnam War, 183–84
  Ali's decision to resist draft, 7, 174, 183–86
  casualties, 165
  McCain and, 38–39
Vision, role in decision-making, 13, 67, 83, 112, 114
Voting Rights Act of 1965, 166

Where the Buck Stops (Truman), 14
Wiesel, Elie, xii, 36–47, 212
  author's meeting with, 42–43
  background of, 41–42
  decision-making lessons of, 47
  decisions during the Holocaust, 6, 36–38, 45
  Madoff scandal and, 43–44
  Night, 36–38, 41–42, 45, 46
  Nobel Peace Prize, 42
Wiesel, Shlomo, 37–38, 41, 45
Wilberforce, William, 167–68, 170, 171
Wittenberg Castle Church, 198
Woods Hole Oceanographic Institution, 139
World War I
  casualties, 165
  Hjalmar Hammarskjöld and, 55–56
  Howard Johnson and, 109
  Joan of Arc and, 74
  Picasso and, 30
World War II, 142
  casualties, 165
  Picasso and, 32
  Truman's decision to use atomic bomb, 3, 6, 11, 12, 17–18
  UN and, 52
  Wiesel and, 36–47

"X rays," 132–33, 135

Yamaguchi, Roy, 113
"Yankee houses," 99
Yousafzai, Malala, 3–4, 205–9, 212
  background of, 205–7
  decision-making lessons of, 208–9
  decision to stand up to Taliban, 8, 205
  Nobel Peace Prize of, 205, 207
Yousafzai, Ziauddin, 205–7

Zwingli, Huldrych, 76